BECOMING A WRITER

STAYING A WRITER

ALSO BY J. MICHAEL STRACZYNSKI

The Complete Book of Scriptwriting
Together We Will Go
Changeling
Babylon 5
Sense8
Rising Stars
Midnight Nation

BECOMING A WRITER

STAYING A WRITER

THE ARTISTRY, JOY, AND CAREER OF STORYTELLING

J. MICHAEL STRACZYNSKI

BenBella Books, Inc.
Dallas, TX

BenBella

BenBella Books, Inc.
10440 N. Central Expressway
Suite 800
Dallas, TX 75231
benbellabooks.com
Send feedback to feedback@benbellabooks.com

BenBella is a federally registered trademark.

Printed in the United States of America
10 9 8 7 6 5 4 3 2 1

Library of Congress Cataloging-in-Publication Control Number: 2020049063
ISBN 9781950665884 (trade paper)
ISBN 9781953295309 (electronic)

Editing by Robb Pearlman
Copyediting by Michael Fedison
Proofreading by Jenny Bridges and Sarah Vostok
Text design and composition by Aaron Edmiston
Cover design by Kara Klontz
Cover image © Shutterstock / Vector FX (text), Le Panda (handwriting), Archi_Viz
   (desktop)
Printed by Versa Press

Special discounts for bulk sales are available.
Please contact bulkorders@benbellabooks.com.

Dedicated—
To you –
Your words, your vision, your voice, your future
And the stories you will tell the world.

And to –
Harlan and Susan Ellison
The former of whom left us on June 28, 2018
And the latter of whom left us
On August 3, 2020
Just as this manuscript was going to press.
If there are words in the dictionary to convey how greatly you are missed
I have not yet found them.

CONTENTS

STAYING A WRITER

INTRODUCTION:
WHY THIS BOOK?

The trick is not becoming a writer. The trick is staying a writer.
Harlan Ellison

As I write these words, I have been fortunate enough to make a living as a writer for over forty years. I've written for newspapers, magazines, anthologies, book publishers, television networks, film studios, and comic companies. My work has found its way into tens of millions of hands worldwide, with the films alone generating over a billion dollars at the box office, and led to far more awards than I probably deserve.

That's where I am *now*. But I *began* this process at the same point, and with the same disadvantage, as everyone else: I was utterly clueless about the process of becoming a writer. Was it a matter of going to the right schools and receiving the right training? Was it about a knack for making connections, or sociability, skills I lacked (and still lack) but which everyone insisted were necessary for pursuing my dreams as a writer? What would it take to get past the guardians at the gate?

Absent useful information, I did what many of those reading this have also done: I listened to advice from people who had never been writers themselves but seemed to know everything about it. The result was a tsunami of misinformation, urban legendry, and myths about writing that

1

failed to intersect with reality at any two contiguous points. But I didn't know that at the time, so I kept running down one wrong path after another, like a man chasing a bus, red-faced and breathing fast, terrified of missing the next connection and getting left behind. As a result, the process of learning how to make a living as a writer took years longer than it should have taken, or *would* have taken, if I'd known what I was doing.

The foregoing experience is not unique to me. Whenever I lecture about writing at workshops, commencement exercises, film schools, universities, and conventions, I spend much of that time correcting false narratives and helping new writers unlearn bad habits. I seek out these conversations because I believe that anyone who achieves success in the arts has a moral obligation to send the elevator down for the next person. I would not be where I am now if not for other writers who served as mentors or examples to study and emulate.

Writing in his anthology *Skeleton Crew*, Stephen King said, "You don't (write) for money, or you're a monkey. You don't think of the bottom line, or you're a monkey. You don't think of it in terms of hourly wage, yearly wage, even lifetime wage, or you're a monkey. In the end you don't even do it for love, although it would be nice to think so. You do it because to *not* do it is suicide."

The reader who understands what King is talking about is the person for whom this volume is most intended. That being said, there are literally thousands of books about writing out there, so why add yet another to the pile? What makes this one worth anyone's time?

For starters, this is not a creative writing textbook. It is intended for those who have already learned the baseline classroom fundamentals, such as: What is a plot? What is dialogue? How do you describe a character? What is the difference between active and passive grammar? How do you use sensory input to enrich narrative description? What are the five stages of a novel? What is the airspeed velocity of an unladen sparrow? (Okay, maybe not that last one.)

Becoming a Writer, Staying a Writer is aimed at writers looking for accurate, practical, and advanced information that can't be found inside the classroom or within the pages of baseline writing books: tips, tricks, and methodologies that are only acquired through years of work.

Writers need to hear different things at various stages of their careers, so the first part of this book is skewed toward beginning writers who need to know what *not* to do as much as what they *should* be doing, techniques and discussions about writing as a craft and a profession that will save them years of wasted effort. The second part leans toward writers who have achieved some measure of success and are eager to get to the next level, refresh their writing skills, or reinvent themselves in order to keep their careers vital and relevant. That being said, there is some overlap between the two parts as they provide information that can be useful to a writer at any stage of his or her development: how to strengthen one's craft and learn the steps needed to make a consistent living as a writer; how the Three Legged Stool Theory can help writers survive economic hardship; how to use the Prince from a Distant Land Scenario to refresh your career; the creative and financial necessity of Craft Rotation; and how to live with creative integrity, deal with notes, and collaborate with another writer, to list just a few examples.

There is one last point that separates this book from other writing texts. As noted in the Stephen King quote, for a true writer, "to not write is suicide." But there's another side to this argument that is more about joy than heartbreak.

There is no drug more powerful, no high more profound, than when the story we are writing reveals itself in unexpected shades of color, meaning, and implication. At that moment the work becomes ecstatic and transformative, no longer a classroom or workshop assignment, but a thing of beauty, birthed in the realization that we can achieve great things when we get out of our own way and surrender to the story. It's only when we become transparent, allowing the work to flow through us like light, unimpeded by ego or the desire to control everything, that we finally understand that one does not *make* art happen; one *lets* art happen.

When we reach that understanding, everything about the writing process becomes beautiful, luminous, and joyful.

That is the life this book is designed to promote: writing as an art, a craft, and a career, but also a source of profound joy.

Every day, I step into my home office where I get to do what I love for a living. Every day, I am surrounded by fascinating people saying the most

BECOMING A WRITER

IN WHICH WE DISCUSS MURDERED TYPEWRITERS, LOST LOVES, AND THE WRITING IMPULSE

little personal background to set the stage.

I began my journey to becoming a writer when I was young and profoundly alone. We moved every six to eight months, traveling all over the country in my family's desperate attempt to avoid creditors and responsibility for, well, *anything*, really, so there was never the time, opportunity, or permission to make friends. To avoid recapitulating the details covered in my autobiography, *Becoming Superman*, I will simply say that it was a horrific childhood that I survived by escaping into books, movies, comics, and Saturday morning cartoons. I had plenty of friends—it's just that none of them actually existed in the real world: Superman and Space Ghost, Johnny Quest and the Jetsons, Tom and Jerry, John Steed and Emma Peel. After that week's window into their worlds closed at the end of the broadcast, I kept the stories going in my head, running off with them on all kinds of adventures. Oh, sure. I couldn't *tell* anyone about them because nobody'd believe me, but to my twelve-year-old brain they were as real as anything else in my world. Realer, even.

I was a chronic daydreamer and consequently a mediocre student, the poor grades on my report cards written in ominous red beside repeated warnings: *Joseph does not apply himself to his studies . . . he spends most of his time looking out the window . . . he is constantly writing things that have nothing to do with completing his assigned work . . . he is inattentive in class . . . his promotion is in danger . . .*

I was malnourished, poorly dressed, socially maladroit, awkward, naïve, and utterly incapable of starting a conversation with anyone, especially girls. It didn't help that I was at the bottom of the social ladder (or more accurately, about a foot *beneath* the social ladder), shunned by the cool kids and beat up by bullies. The degree to which I was the school's resident pariah was brought home to me in sixth grade, when I slipped a Valentine's Day card into the locker of a girl I liked. When she found it, she tracked me down, knocked me to the floor, and began kicking the crap out of me. Coming from a family noted for domestic violence, I had taken a blood oath, still unbroken, against *ever* raising my hand to a woman, under any circumstances, even in self-defense, so I just took it as everyone looked on and laughed.

Despite such incidents, I remained a hopeless romantic, my nascent writing skills spinning endless stories in my head about the day the Perfect Girl would come into my life, someone who could see past the shoddy clothes and nervous mannerisms to the real person inside. As much as writers like to dream about distant worlds and exotic places, our Secret Truth is that we also use our words to seek out affection and empathy, and I very much needed to believe that I would someday be worthy of someone's love. The more I surrendered to those stories, to that *hope*, the more I became convinced that the Perfect Girl was out there somewhere—I just needed to find her and figure out how to actually *talk* to her.

In ninth grade, the school held a Computer Dance. Students filled out forms listing their interests, height, goals, and other useful information that was transferred to punch cards and fed into a computer that would match Student A to Student B. As someone who believed in the power of science, I thought, *Finally, someone has come up with a logical, foolproof way to identify the Perfect Girl! I won't have to try and introduce myself or impress her because we're already a pair; science said so! I have to go!*

Normally I was forbidden to take part in after-hours school activities (and the bullies didn't help matters), but my father was out of town that week, so I filled in the form and watched as the data was punched into long cards and stacked alongside the others. *She's in there somewhere, waiting for me!*

The night of the dance, I cleaned up as best I could, found a shirt that wasn't too badly worn, and walked the two miles to school. (We weren't on a regular bus line and the school buses didn't operate at night. Everyone else was dropped off by their parents.) At a long table outside the gymnasium, I picked up a blue card bearing my ID number (83) and the number of my date (105), safety-pinned it to my shirt, and walked inside. The gym was festooned with streamers, handmade posters, and brightly colored light-wheels that were normally only dragged out for Christmas. The place was packed, the music pounding as I made my way through the crowd in search of #105. In my head the story of our meeting played out as a moment of mutual, soulful recognition; we would step outside to talk, I would tell her about wanting to be a writer, she would confide her own dreams, and from that day forward we would walk to and from school together, sharing lunches and confidences and, in time, perhaps even a kiss.

I'm here, I thought. *I'll find you; wait for me!*

I searched for half an hour, but #105 was nowhere to be seen. *Maybe there was an emergency and she had to go home,* I thought, *or maybe the car broke down on the way here and she's not coming.*

Then, for just a moment, the crowd parted, and I saw a bright red paper circle stamped with the number 105 pinned to a black-and-white skirt. I pushed through the bodies on the dance floor, desperate not to lose track of her. Then with one final lunge I was there, in front of *Her,* at last.

And I froze.

At the time of this story, I was barely five feet four inches tall.

She was at least five-ten, and a year or two ahead of me.

But the computer had said this was her, *my* her, and years of reading science fiction stories had taught me that science was always right, so I stepped up and tried to make my mouth work. Nothing came out. She was so busy talking with her girlfriends that it took a moment before she noticed me staring up at her. *"What?!"* she said, glaring at me like something unpleasant she'd found on the bottom of her shoe.

I could've said anything. I could've said, *My name's Joe.* I could've said, *You look great,* or *I was looking for you,* or even just *Hi*—anything that might have induced her to see me as an actual person. Instead, I plucked the card marked #83 from my shirt, held it up in front of me like a frightened villager fending off a vampire, and squeaked out, "Eighty-three!"

When she didn't hear or seem to get it, I said it again. Twice. Just that. *Eighty-three!*

Then she checked her *Your Match Is . . .* card and her face flushed red. "Ewww," she said, then tore the card into six pieces, threw them on the floor, and stalked off with her friends in search of someone, *anyone,* who was not me.

Telling that story pains me almost as much as it does to admit that I'm *still* socially inept. When I'm writing a scene, the character who is standing in for me has no problem talking to others, challenging them, or even flirting, because I know in advance what the character on the receiving end of that conversation is going to say in response. But in real life I never know what the other person will say, or how they will expect me to respond in turn, and that is a fearsome prospect for someone who is just *thismuch* on the spectrum. *Stick with the imaginary conversations, pal, where there's at least a chance of you actually initiating an adult conversation.*

Eighty-three!

In furtherance of the preceding, pre-italicized point: I spent the years 2001–2002 in Vancouver, Canada, show-running a TV series for Showtime entitled *Jeremiah*. Despite being newly single, I was living absolutely alone, without any attachments or relationships. I wasn't even *trying* to date. When the crew discovered what was (or technically wasn't) going on, all of them suddenly had opinions about how I should be spending my free time. This included another producer who pulled me aside to recommend a showbiz mixer that took place monthly at a local restaurant/club. "You should go. It's always twice as many women as guys, so it's a good place to find somebody."

By this time I'd acquired a solid reputation in television. I'd been a show-runner and written hundreds of scripts, I'd won all kinds of awards . . . I was, like, a *guy,* you know? The Romantic Storyteller in my head immediately began spinning out scenarios in which I rolled into the club all charm and accomplishment and *hey, hi, so what's your name?*

I attended every mixer over the next four months.

And never spoke to anyone.

Not once.

Soda in hand, I would circle the room along the edges, sometimes daring to walk through the crowd to the other side, then repeat the pattern for an hour or two before escaping into the night. On the long walk back to my apartment just off Granville Island, I justified my failure to connect on the grounds that I'm too polite for my own good, and didn't want to interrupt women who were busy talking to their friends and having fun. And there is truth to that. Other nights, I chalked it up to being in awe of women, who I've always seen as smarter, funnier, better conversationalists, and infinitely more aware and awake than most men. And there's truth to *that* as well.

But the core of it was the simple fact that I had absolutely no idea how to walk up and introduce myself to someone who exists in a world outside my own head. I *still* don't know how to do it, which is why I am terrible at making friends.

But I'm really good at *creating* them.

That's what writers do for a living: we create *friends*, people we want to hang out with, good guys and bad guys and people in-between who are brighter and hipper and funnier and better dressed and a hell of a lot more interesting than we will *ever* be, but they let us hang around because they need us to type up all the cool things they're about to do.

We create people and worlds and adventures because there's something about the story of *this* world that we don't like or understand, that makes us feel like we don't fit in or that there's something important that we alone can fix. Going back to Stephen King's statement, writing is as much a state of mind as it is a profession, and the psychology of that process invariably begins when we are very young, long before we start to consciously zero in on anything resembling craft. Storytelling allows us to disappear from this reality into one of our own design that's both safer (because we control it) and more dangerous (because when we are being honest in our storytelling, we never *really* know what it will reveal about our characters or ourselves). Writing is our escape route to a place where things make sense because we have the author's power to *force* them to make sense.

And there are all kinds of consequences to that single-minded escape.

Poor grades and apocalyptic warnings notwithstanding, I passed through high school unknown, unseen, and unremarked upon until my senior year, when two teachers glimpsed the writer inside and decided to do all they could to encourage me to step into the light. This led to me and several other students being enlisted by Creative Writing teacher JoAnn Massie to pen stories, essays, and poems for *Under the Sun*, a mimeographed school magazine. (A mimeograph was an early process for making multiple copies of a document that used inked sheets sandwiched between two pages to stencil out illustrations as they were being drawn, or letters as they were being typed, and which were then inserted into the mimeo machine for reproduction.) The writing was to be done in her classroom after regular school hours.

Most of the students wrote their offerings by hand, but since I and a few others knew how to type, Massie said that we could bring in typewriters. But my father refused to let me drag the monstrous machine we had at home to the school via bus, so Massie brought one of her own into class for me to use.

I should mention that the classroom desks used at this time were made of aluminum with a thin desktop that curved around from the side, and plastic seats above a slender bookrack. They were light enough to be quickly moved into a circle for group discussions, then returned just as easily to their proper rows. This will become important in a moment.

I was seated at the front of the room, a pile of mimeograph paper in front of me, as Massie set the typewriter that she had brought from home down on my desk. "Good luck," she said with a smile, and moved off to chat with other students. I fed in a sheet of paper, checked several times to be sure that it went in straight, meticulously adjusted the margins, and began writing a short story entitled "Chant of the Dead." I was very much in my Lovecraft period, so the writing was painfully derivative of his style. During their early development, writers try on writing styles the way other people try on shoes, looking for the perfect fit. So I went through a Poe stage, a Lovecraft stage, a Hunter Thompson stage . . . it's what we do.

Despite its clichéd Lovecraftian influences and rank superficiality (I even named the town in the story Markham because Arkham would have been way too obvious), I escaped into the story to the exclusion of everything around me. The world consisted of me and the story and nothing else, as if I were the only person in the room.

When I hit the end of the page, I pulled it out and reached for the next one, only to discover that the inked page between the two sheets had been damaged. The remaining sheets shared similar issues. Then I glanced over at a table across the room where writing supplies had been set up and saw a pile of mimeo sheets that looked intact.

Thinking only of where I was in the story and what I wanted—no, *needed*—to write next, I stood up from my desk and headed toward the table.

I'd barely gone three steps when, out of the corner of my eye, I saw my lightweight desk starting to tilt forward under the weight of the typewriter. It seemed to be going almost in slow motion, like the *Titanic* starting its long descent into the deep. Then gravity overcame inertia, and in the instant before I could reach it, the desk flipped upside down, throwing the typewriter to the floor. It shattered into a spray of shift keys, vowels, and consonants, the ribbon spiraling in one direction as the cylinder bounced out of its cradle and slammed into the wall hard enough to cause a dent.

No one moved. No one spoke. Massie's frozen expression betrayed a look of horror as intense as anything ever seen in a John Carpenter movie.

I prayed for death. It went unanswered.

"I'm sorry," I stammered out, fighting tears. "I'm sorry, I—"

"No, it's . . . it's okay, Joe," Massie said when she could finally speak. "It's not your fault—accidents happen, and I . . . I wasn't using that one a lot anyway; it wasn't my primary typewriter. So don't think two things about it. I have another typewriter at home. I'll bring that one in tomorrow, and you can finish then."

With that, we began to collect the pieces of the shattered typewriter, gamely trying to figure out what parts went where, even though we all knew it had been destroyed beyond repair.

I felt like an assassin.

The next day I was back at my desk, a fresh stack of flawless mimeo sheets in hand as Massie placed an even larger and heavier typewriter down before me. The beast seemed to weigh at least as much as I did, so as I began writing I planted my feet ahead of me and sat back firmly to ensure that there would be no recurrence of the previous day's trauma.

I reached the end of the story without incident, then spent another little while proofreading the pages and making corrections. Once that was done, still wrapped up in the story to the exclusion of all else, I managed a single real-world thought—*Okay, I should show this to Mrs. Massie for her approval*—and rose to walk the story over to her.

This time I didn't see it happen. I heard only the scream from one of the students as the desk flipped forward with such velocity that it bounced twice before slamming into the cabinet at the front of the room. The typewriter hit the floor keys-first and exploded like a grenade, sending shrapnel in every direction.

I had murdered two typewriters in two days.

Massie turned slowly toward me, her hands covering her mouth to keep from screaming as every conceivable emotion flashed through her wide eyes. *He's an idiot I'm going to kill him I don't want to traumatize him I'll break his neck how can anyone be so stupid this was my father's typewriter I'm going to wring his—*

"It's okay," she said at last, her voice weaker and significantly less convincing than the day before. "It's . . . it was an *accident*, and accidents . . . *happen*. It's . . . it's okay."

After we finished removing the body, I explained that the reason I'd gotten up was to bring her the finished story. "I guess I just kind of got lost in it," I said.

She took the pages, started back to her desk, then stopped abruptly in mid-step.

"There's a mistake," she said, pointing to the top of the first page. "The title and your name are supposed to be up here."

"I know," I said. "But I wasn't sure I could get it done right, so I figured I'd try to write it first and if I liked it enough, then I'd put the title and my name on it."

"Well, it needs to be there, so it'll match the format everyone else is using."

I nodded absently for a moment, then said, very softly, "If you want it to look consistent with what's already on the page, I'll need another typewriter." ·

She looked at me.

I looked at her.

A tumbleweed blew through the room.

"Nooooo, in this case I think it'll be fine if you just handwrite it," she said, and handed back the pages.

Writing isn't just what we do, it's who we *are*; it's who we have always been and will always be, on an almost cellular level. We spend our days observing and cataloging and listening and logging and making connections between ideas and images and random words until suddenly a story appears and the outer world disappears because at that moment nothing else matters. This has led me to the altogether subjective conclusion that writers are born, not made. Yes, technique can be taught; anyone can be made a *better* writer, maybe even a *skilled* writer, but learning how to structure a sentence for maximum impact is very different from the storytelling impulse that drives writers from cradle to grave, overriding everything else in our lives until it becomes more necessary and more profoundly consequential than the need for food, shelter, love, or human company.

This single-minded focus on escaping the real world for the one where stories live has served me well on many occasions. It allowed me to single-handedly write 92 out of 110 produced episodes of *Babylon 5*, a record unmatched by any other member of the Writers Guild of America, along with hundreds of comics, and entire screenplays in little to no time when the studio or publisher needed the job done quickly.

On the other hand, whenever I've been fortunate enough to go out on a date, usually at the invitation of the other party, sooner or later will come a moment when the conversation is going great, there's fun and laughter and deep sub-referencing going on, I'll look off into the distance for what I think is just a second—

—and when I rack focus back into the booth and the table and the moment, the woman sitting across from me will note that I haven't said anything in a long, long, *really* long time.

"Where did you go?" she will ask. "Because you sure as hell weren't *here*."

Where did I go?

I went to the place where stories live when they demand to be told.

I don't have much choice in the matter. I go where I'm kicked.

If you put a bunch of writers in a room and one of them starts talking about how the people in their head have always felt more real and substantive than anyone else they know, and how the work is constantly pulling them against their will into all the deep places where stories abide, the rest will nod their heads in recognition. *Yeah, that's how it is for me, too,* they will say, like members of a twelve-step program admitting to a unique and unshakeable addiction that they can't share with others because (a) they wouldn't understand and (b) most of us are still figuring out that whole making-direct-eye-contact thing with non-writers.

So, if you, gentle reader, also found yourself nodding with painful familiarity as you made your way through the preceding pages . . . congratulations—you've found the right book.

One doesn't *have* to be a socially maladroit loner with a penchant for daydreaming and a roster of friends who exist only in one's head to be a writer, but to be honest, that *does* describe a lot of us. But it's also possible to be all those things and *not* be a writer. So what makes the difference? Whence the Rubicon?

I think it starts with the belief that we have something to say that may actually be worth *listening* to. As a kid who was always being told to shut up, written off as a dead-ender by family and teachers alike, I was determined to show the doubters that I had an important story to tell, one that would change the world. That obsession is sometimes necessary to carry us through periods of self-doubt, but it can also result in the Great American Novel complex that paralyzes so many writers. Sure enough, every time I tried to make the work sound important, it came out the other side pompous, pretentious, portentous, self-indulgent, and stuffy. Desperate for acceptance and applause, I kept bending the writing impulse to the *result* rather than embracing the *process*, more focused on how I wanted the world to *perceive* the work than on the quality of the work itself.

It took me years to realize that my priorities were upside down.

It's not about writing something important, it's about writing something *true*, and truth rarely shouts its importance. It tends to speak very softly, and only if it's sure you're listening.

Early atomic bomb tests produced massive explosions. But what made those explosions *happen* was a small amount of explosives placed with care at the center of the device. This triggered a chain reaction that ignited the fissionable material, which *then* spiraled into a massive detonation. Take away that tiny, painfully precise explosion at the center, and the big event would never happen. As I made my way into television writing, I began to realize that truth in storytelling works much the same way. Instead of trying to yell out a big truth, it's sometimes better to put a small but relatable truth at the center of what you're creating in the hope of igniting the fissionable material of the human heart, thereby triggering an explosion of empathy, self-reflection, and understanding.

The smaller the truth, the more universal it is, because we all have experience with small but potent truths; by contrast, the bigger and grander the statement, the less universally applicable it can become. People rarely talk in profundities; most of the time they speak in small but deeply personal truths that are less about the Meaning of Life than what it felt like when the last of their grandparents passed away.

This understanding crystallized into something practicable during my tenure as the executive story editor on a reboot of *The Twilight Zone*. I was having dinner with friend and mentor Harlan Ellison (from whose tutelage the title of this volume is derived), and hit him with a question about a script I was writing.

"The main character's wife died in an accident several years earlier," I said, "and he's still not over the grief. He's tormented by the fact that the last time they talked, the conversation turned into an argument, so I'm looking for something interesting they can argue about. Maybe he thinks she's spending too much money, or there's a political argument, or they're behind on rent, or one of them suspects the other is having an affair . . . I've tried a bunch of different subjects but none of them seem to work, so I thought you might have a suggestion."

"Those are certainly all big arguments," Harlan said.

"Yeah," I said, failing to perceive the trap that was being set before me. "I think it needs to be something substantive."

"And that's *exactly* why it's not working," he said. "Arguments like the ones you described happen all the time, and they're just standard TeeVee stuff. Yeah, he'd feel bad about arguing with her before she died, but he wouldn't necessarily *regret* it on a very personal basis because rent *happens*, bills *happen.* You know what we regret? We regret all the really stupid things we've done, the stuff that comes out of nowhere to haunt us while we're sitting at a stoplight waiting for the green.

"So, instead of arguing about rent, how about this: You know those jars of cherry or plum preserves you get at breakfast? He always called them jams but to be cute and funny she called them jellies instead, so every morning for the last thirty years he'd say, 'Pass the jam, dear,' and she'd say, 'Here's the jelly, dear.' Then one day he was in a bad mood—maybe he didn't get a good night's sleep or there's something else bothering him—and when she says, 'Here's the jelly, dear,' he just goes off on her, saying that after thirty freaking years it's not funny, it's never *been* funny, and when he asks for the goddamned jam just give him the goddamned jam and stop giving him crap about it.

"They finish breakfast in that stony, post-argument silence, and he knows he overreacted but he has to get to work so he figures he'll apologize later. But she gets killed in an accident that afternoon and *later* never happens. So it's not just that they argued, it's that it was a *stupid* argument because he was being an ass, and unfair, and petty, and he'd give *anything* to have those five minutes back so he could make it right."

Not rent. Not politics. Not affairs. Because that's just *stuff* people argue about all the time and sometimes it's nobody's fault. Jams and jellies. Because on a core emotional level we understand how deeply we'd regret having an argument that petty, stupid, and unnecessary with a loved one on the last day of their life.

That was the afternoon the words *If You Want to Go Big, Go Small* were forever etched behind my eyes.

Much of my work since then has been about finding tiny truths that needn't be heavy or ponderous. I once wrote a TV episode about two characters in a shuttle going from point A to point B in space. They have six hours to kill before they arrive, and no distractions other than the view out the window. So when one of them wants to break the long, awkward silence, instead of talking about the Big Stuff, about forthcoming battles or other matters of importance, he asks, "So: fasten-zip or zip-fasten?"

When the other character asks what the hell he's talking about, he explains that when people put their pants on, some zip first then fasten the top button, while others fasten the top button first and *then* zip. Thanks to that question, not only did the main character have to think about it, every viewer watching the episode *also* had to think about it, and discuss it with their friends the next day, and to this day, *twenty years after that conversation aired*, whenever I appear at a convention someone will raise his or her hand during the question-and-answer part of the program and say, "So, Joe . . . fasten or zip?"

As to where I am now on this journey, after years spent chasing truths big and small, I've come to the conclusion that the core explosive element at the center of a story is subtler and more elegant than I'd thought. Yes, truth is a big part of it, but it is not the *whole* of it, or the purpose of it.

It's about creating beauty.

Beauty is what we seek when we enter a movie theater or turn on the television. We want to be entertained, yes, but also uplifted and ennobled. Our eyes grow soft when we see art, music, and unexpected beauty. The whirl of the ballet, the perfect concluding note, the seemingly effortless made possible only by years of struggle for perfection in line and form. Beauty enriches us, making us aspire to be better than we imagined possible, and it has great power.

While working on a screenplay set in a Gypsy concentration camp during World War Two, I spoke with a man who claimed descent from one of those who helped design the camps, for which there were two essential rules:

First, that there was nowhere anyone could go inside the camp without being seen by guards in the towers or on the ground.

Second, that there could be no beauty, anywhere.

Because beauty leads to hope, and hope leads to insurrection.

Truth *in*forms us and tells us who we are; beauty *trans*forms us and tells us what we can *be*.

As a boy trapped in awful circumstances, I longed for beauty; daydreamed of beauty; struggled to escape to beauty; was awed into shy silence by beauty; and, without consciously realizing it, have spent a lifetime in the pursuit of beauty.

Beauty is the first impulse and the last destination in a writer's journey, because only in the latter stage does its essential nature reveal itself in ways that can be understood and acted upon. So though I still aspire to the truth, the most recent years of my career have been dedicated to the pursuit of beauty in storytelling.

And there is no greater beauty in all the world than seeing new voices, and new art, arise in places where they had not been seen before. New dreamers. New stories.

New writers.

Like you.

You are just being born, and no matter what you may feel to the contrary, you are beautiful.

Deal with it.

WHO ARE YOU?

VERSION 1.0

Let's turn the camera around to focus on you, your family, and your ambitions.

In one scenario, your parents, relatives, and friends believe in you. They want you to succeed, to tell your stories and make your art. They support your efforts emotionally and financially, and dream of one day walking into a bookstore or a theater or turning on the TV to see your name right there in front of them.

If so, congratulations. You are one of a relatively small number of aspiring writers who fall into this category, because most people end up in . . .

Scenario Two, wherein your friends and family (a) don't believe you have what it takes, (b) would rather see you get a degree in something that (theoretically) guarantees you a job, or (c) agree that you might have some talent but the odds against success are huge. Determined to try and protect you from the prospect of failure, humiliation, and poverty, they will do everything possible to deflect you into a different path, a *proper* job where with luck you *might* be able to pursue your art as a lesser priority.

Since Scenario One attends to itself, let's drill a little deeper into Scenario Two.

The Gospel According to Mark, 6:4, reads, "A prophet is not without honor, save in his own country, and among his own kin, and in his own house." Meaning: It's easier to impress strangers than those who grew up with you, who *knew you when*, as the saying goes. Writers, like other artists, are considered magical creatures who spring into existence somewhere *out there* in the vast unknown; they're not someone's dopey brother or silly sister. Knowing too well who you *were* prevents your friends and family from seeing who you *are* and what you're *becoming*, leading them to react with skepticism, concern, or sarcasm. *Who do you think you are? What makes you think you're so special?*

A writer is without honor only in his or her own home, among his or her own family.

Overcoming self-doubt is difficult enough; pursuing your art in the face of doubt or downright opposition by friends and family is one of the hardest things for a beginning writer to achieve. You (presumably) love your family; you've trusted them and looked to them for guidance for your entire life; if they think you don't have what it takes, there's an impulse to think that maybe they're right and you should listen to them.

But even if your family and friends *do* agree that you have some rough-hewn talent, they're still going to be terrified that you'll fail. They're not against you, they love you, want the best for you, and don't want to see you get hurt, so for what they see as your own good, your own *protection*, they four-wall you with soft discouragement. *What if it doesn't work out? What if you end up nowhere and you've wasted all that time? How are you going to make a living at this? The odds are against you. Maybe you should try something else.*

I refer to this as the Tyranny of Reasonable Voices, which is motivated as much by fear of failure as it is by love, because to fail, especially to fail *publicly*, is society's ultimate taboo. But we cannot achieve anything of value unless we are willing to fail in the process. Military tacticians argue that failure is necessary from time to time because it helps you locate the vulnerabilities in your armor or the weaknesses in the campaign. You try to get over the wall, fail, figure out what you did wrong, and apply those lessons to get over it the next time.

It's a peculiar truth that success as a writer is often determined by one's willingness to embrace his inner failure.

Artists make their art, sell their art, then move on to the next piece. The problem with being a writer is that what we make doesn't actually exist in the real world—it's not a piece of physical art, a one-off widget or a nicely made cabinet. We sit staring into the distance, making stuff up. This is counterintuitive to a society based on the notion that you must have a *job*, go to an *office*, where you make a *thing*, and get a regular *paycheck*, with (maybe, if they feel like it) *benefits* and some measure of *security* (which is an illusion under the best of circumstances, but that's a topic for another book). After earning a living as a writer for ten years, I *still* had relatives asking when I was going to get a real job.

Everyone comes out of high school armed with dreams about their future, and at some point we have to decide between following those dreams and taking the path of least resistance. Giving up one's dreams on the grounds that the odds against achieving them are substantial is simpler than putting oneself on the line, and it lets everyone *else* off the hook as well. Because if you decide to follow your dreams and actually manage to achieve some measure of success, it calls into question the decisions made by those around you not to do the same. Demonstrating that what they insisted was impossible *is* possible shifts the focus to their own lack of courage, and nobody wants to face that. Consequently, there are some who will always do everything possible to discourage you from following *your* dreams as justification for them not following *theirs*.

Which brings us back to the question of what *you* want, what you hope to achieve, and your doubts—personal or secondhand—about whether or not you will be able to reach those goals. Beginning writers often find themselves torn between the two poles of *I really want to make this work* and *I don't know if I have the talent to make this work.*[1] Eager for validation, they keep hoping someone will come along to say, *Yes, you have undeniable talent and will absolutely be successful—go forth with confidence.* But success can never be predicted with surety, and anyone who says otherwise is trying to sell you something. Usually a book on writing.

The other awful thing about being a writer[2] is that we spend the first half of our lives trying to convince people that we have talent, and the

---

1 This feeling never entirely goes away, regardless of accomplishment; it only changes form. Every experienced writer starts his or her next novel thinking, "How am I going to make this story fill 500 pages?" followed at the midpoint by, "How the hell am I going to fit all this into just 500 pages?"

2 Aren't you glad you bought this book?

second half trying to convince *ourselves*. Since that process never really ends, you might as well get used to the pain now and save yourself years of therapy later.

Absent guarantees of talent as a writer, there are only prospects and probabilities, signs, portents, and characteristics that can indicate you're on the right path. The traits vary depending on where you are in your development, but in general they look like this:

Maybe you're in high school, and instead of throwing around a football, firing up the latest version of *Call of Duty*, or going out with friends, you spend most of your time at home, writing stories or poems or journal entries. You write them because something inside you *has* to write them, but also because it's fun; you enjoy it when the words take you places you've never been before, revealing secrets no one else will ever truly understand. On the other hand, you're not entirely sure if you have the courage to show your words to the world because they contain ideas and thoughts you rarely express out loud because that's your style; for every six thoughts that flit through your mind, you only give voice to one or two. People say you live too much inside your own head, and maybe that's true, but it's a lot more interesting in there than the world outside.

Maybe you've just started college and the edges of your world have broadened in profound, life-altering ways. Until now, other people got to decide what classes you should take, what tests you had to pass, and which hoops you had to jump through. The table before you was set with few options, none of which you had any control over. The same meals day in and day out. Now, suddenly, you're in a banquet hall filled with unimagined possibilities, a riot of tastes, textures, and colors, and while that is exciting and liberating it can also be frightening and more than a little confusing. The classes over *there* are the ones your parents and academic advisors *want* you to take, the ones you *promised* you would take to get that safe, reliable job in science, law, or accounting; but the classes over *here* are the ones that truly excite you: creative writing, crafting short stories, writing for the stage and for television. The head knows which classes lead to sensible results, but the heart knows what the heart needs . . . and it sure as hell ain't accounting.[3]

Maybe you can't afford college, so you're trying to survive the gig economy by working multiple jobs, whipsawed between shifts at unpredictable hours for crap money and no benefits, knowing you can be fired at any time without recourse. Lacking stability, unable to stop and catch your breath, you go through your days and nights like Alice in the Mad Queen's Race, running as fast as you can just to stay in one place. There's no time for anything except work, sleep, and despair. But, despite the fatigue, you force yourself to set aside a few moments in the morning, or between shifts, or during lunch to pull out a small notepad and jot down lines of verse, dialogue, or plot . . . sketches and ideas . . . little acts of creative resistance that make you happy and keep you sane despite the lunatic hours.

Alternatively, perhaps the linear path of university study isn't something you want or need to pursue. You work as a contractor or a fine carpenter, a photographer or a musician; you own a small business or work as a medical tech; or maybe you're a bit lost, eyes locked on the far horizon, trying to figure out your path through the world. But none of that precludes the ever-growing sense deep inside that you have something to say that might have a profound effect on the world.[4]

Finally, maybe you're older in years but still young in your desire to tell stories. Your regular job has served you well; you have a family and responsibilities and lately the days flash by so fast that they're gone before you even know they showed up. You didn't pursue your art earlier in life because you were drowned under a flood-tide of commitments and uncertainties, but by now you've experienced enough of life to be on surer footing with yourself and your ideas. There are things you want to say that you didn't know

---

3 Which is not to say there's anything wrong with being an accountant. Not at all. Accounting is a fine and honorable and noble profession. I say this because it is true, because it is fair, and because I do not wish to be audited should this book find its way into the hands of someone easily offended at the business management firm that handles my accounts.

4 A decision not to attend college doesn't have to be an impediment to your success as a writer, as evidenced by such folks as Ray Bradbury, Truman Capote, Maya Angelou, Jack Kerouac, and William Faulkner.

how to express before, or were worried might not be acceptable to those around you. But as the road before you shortens every day, the need to say those things intensifies, and you study the lists of writers who started late in life—James Michener and Sherwood Anderson, Laura Ingalls Wilder and Helen DeWitt, Charles Bukowski and Raymond Chandler—in the hope that someday a similar list might have your name on it. It's late in the day and you're not sure if you have the strength and the talent and the time to get from here to there, but you want . . . *need* . . . to try.

If any of the preceding descriptions resonate with you, then we have much to discuss.

Let's begin.

WRITING FOR THE WORKSHOP

omposer and satirist Tom Lehrer once said, "Life is like a sewer. What you get out of it depends a great deal on what you put into it." Much the same can be said of baseline college-level creative writing classes. On the one hand, they provide an invaluable service by introducing students to the fundamental principles of writing, teaching metaphor and simile, ways to improve grammatical clarity, and how to plot fiction or craft a poem. The quality of our thoughts is bordered on all sides by our facility with language, so learning to express oneself clearly and creatively makes the mind sharper and more resilient.

The flipside is that entry-level classes can be of limited use to students who actually aspire to become writers, or can even work *against* that goal if the instructors focus on telling students how they *should* write rather than looking at how they *do* write in order to help them transfer those unique voices onto the written page. Forcing students to conform to preconceived notions of a particular literary style can make the more creative souls among us feel self-conscious or penned in, trapped between what they want to say and the potentially restrictive way the instructor will allow them to say it. This can cause beginning writers to become discouraged or lose interest, or create bad habits that can take years to unlearn. The teaching process should be about *shedding* preconceived notions about writing, not adding more to the pile.

Good writing is nothing more or less than speaking on the page in one's own natural voice, then editing those words until they are as specific and precise as a laser. This can best be illustrated by a conversation that took place over lunch between science fiction writer Isaac Asimov and his agent. The still-young and struggling Asimov confessed to being near despair about how he should be writing. His concerns were less about plotting and character development than the actual process of laying down the words so they sounded right, sounded *literary*.

The agent nodded silently for a moment. It was a concern he'd heard many times before. "Isaac," he said at last, "do you know how Hemingway would write, *The sun rose in the morning?*"

"No," Asimov said, hoping for revelation. "How?"

"*The sun rose in the morning.* You just say it, that's all."

You just say it. Four words, one syllable each, but some writers spend decades chasing their implications.

Creative writing classes should encourage students to express themselves freely. There is a profound joy to be found in watching those who were shushed into silence one time too many come out the other side with a new sense of purpose, agency, and value. But that joy quickly evaporates if the classroom experience turns into a tightly controlled fiefdom in which the instructor insists that his or her preferred model of writing is the *only* way to write properly, penalizing the independently minded while rewarding those who learn to parrot that model or otherwise curry favor. This is problematic on several levels, especially since grading creative works is a highly subjective process. If you get graded incorrectly for an answer on a history or math test, you can appeal to the department head; if the instructor says a short piece was written badly—by his or her personal standards—there's no recourse for an objective intervention.

Early in my college experience, I was taking a class in creative writing from an instructor who seemed to have issues with women who chose to speak their minds and follow their own voices rather than doing what he told them to do, in the way he told them to do it. This was reflected both in his grading process—male students tended to do a bit better than the female students—and his manner during class. He called on male students more frequently and was more encouraging to them, and regarded the female students with imperious impatience, often critiquing their work with unnecessary brusqueness.

One afternoon, while discussing stories submitted the week before, he lit into one of the female students in ways that I felt were not only unduly harsh but inappropriate. He seemed to *enjoy* berating her, and since his position precluded her from talking back or challenging him on his behavior, he kept pushing until she was literally in tears.

Then from the back of the room a voice called out, very firmly and very coldly, "Leave her the hell alone."[1]

I was as surprised as anyone else to realize it was me.

He flushed an angry red and suggested we take this outside.

"Fine by me," I said, and out we went.

His conduct once we were on the other side of the door led me to believe that he was trying to provoke me into a fight so he could get me expelled. Refusing to take the bait, I made sure my hands never left my pockets as I repeated my assertion that his behavior was inappropriate, and that he owed her an apology.

He declined and took the matter to other members of the department in the hope of bringing the walls of Jericho down around my head. But they refused to get involved, their attitude best reflected by a quote from the play and movie *Man of La Mancha*, "Kill each other if you must, but for god's sake do it quietly."

Prior to the events of that afternoon, I had been receiving high marks in his class for my work. Afterward, my grades dropped to Ds and the occasional D-minus. I think he would have gone for Fs but that would have drawn too much attention and set the stage for an appeal.

On the last day of the term, as I walked toward the door, he stepped in front of me and said, loud enough for everyone else to hear, "You'll *never* be a writer, Mr. Straczynski. You don't have the disposition for it."

---

1 *Hell* was not actually the word applied in that sentence. I use it here only to ensure viability in certain bookstores. Suffice to say it was a word I have never used before or since when addressing an instructor.

Later, when I began publishing articles and other works, I made it a point to send copies to his office, just to annoy him.[2] He never responded. After a while there were too many pieces to keep doing this consistently, so I stopped. A few years thereafter, I learned that he had passed away. Feeling the need to pay my respects, I found out where he had been buried, went to the site of his grave, wrapped my most recent article around a pencil, and shoved it into the ground above where I estimated his heart would be, just in case he tried to rise again.

Not that I hold a grudge.

Despite this experience, I continued taking creative writing classes— some of them very general while others dealt with one specific form of fiction or another—on the assumption that this was the best way to acquire the tools I needed to become a writer. I discovered that I was on the wrong path after taking yet another class in Short Story Writing at San Diego State University. I'd had such a good time learning from the instructor, Richard E. Kim, that I eagerly signed up the following semester for his lecture class on Writing the Novel. But as I approached my desk on day one, he saw me and pulled me out into the hallway.

"You've learned everything I can teach you, and I've taught you everything I know," he said. "What you have to learn now can't be learned by me talking to you about writing. It can only be discovered through the writing itself, and that means taking some really intense workshops."

And with that, he booted me out.

It was the best thing he could possibly have done for me, because he was right. Writers learn to write by writing, and workshops force students to write tons of material, then submit the work not just to the teacher but to the entire class for a group critique. Workshops are necessary at this stage in a writer's development because the safe training wheels of a lecture class will never get you where you need to go. That can only come by entering an arena filled with your peers, in a more even-handed

---

2 When I became friends with Harlan Ellison many years later, I discovered that he'd had a similar bad experience with a writing teacher and fought back in much the same way, for the same reason: our own personal amusement. On hearing this revelation I suggested that we were "twins, separated at mirth." For several days afterward, he refused to come to the phone if he knew it was me on the line.

gestalt between the students and the instructor. This is infinitely preferable to asking friends and family members for opinions of your work because they will rarely tell you what they really think, and even if they are inclined toward honesty, they lack the training and terminology needed to explain where you might have gone astray.

The prospect of having one's work critiqued by twenty relative strangers can be daunting for young writers who are already insecure about the quality of their work, but workshops can create an environment that is positive and supportive provided that the participants agree to provide *constructive* criticism. This doesn't mean soft-pedaling your reaction to a given work, but it does require fairness and precision. You don't say a story is *bad* just because *you* don't like it; literary sensibilities vary, and a story that doesn't appeal to you may find a wide audience elsewhere. Such critiques are not only useless, their subjectivity gives the recipient permission to simply wave away any concerns. *There's nothing wrong with my story—you just don't like it. That's your opinion and mine is mine.* Participants must be able to explain *why* they don't like something, not just announce *that* they don't like it. What *specifically* about the story was bothersome? Was the grammar off? The protagonist unlikeable? The plot contrived? The ending forced or unrealistic? The more precise and objective the critique, the more your fellow students will be forced to address the *work* instead of addressing *you*.

Constructive criticism can sound like this: "I can see you put a lot of work into this, and there are some nice beats to it. I liked the supporting characters, and the writing style was tight. What didn't work, at least for me, was the motivation of the main character. You say—or more accurately *he* says—that he's killing all these people to avenge his brother's murder. But we never actually see the murder, or how he and his brother got along before that happened. So if you want us to understand the extreme steps he's taking to be the avenging angel, I feel like it's important to see them together before the murder. It's not enough for the character to just say it as a plot point or a rationalization for the audience; we should *feel* the reasons for what he does, and we can only do that if you connect the dots. It's clear that *you* know what happened, that you have all these really great scenes in your head, so my suggestion would be to move some of those scenes from the implied to the seen, either at the beginning of the story or, if you feel strongly about the need to hit the ground running, then maybe in flashbacks or transitional pieces between some of the action sequences. Anyway, that's my two cents, and I'd be curious to know if anyone else in the group felt the same way, or if they felt that the implied relationship between the brothers was strong enough that seeing it would be redundant."

The importance of critiquing your fellow students fairly becomes apparent when it's your turn in the barrel. If you treated them appropriately, they will return the favor. If you haven't, then you're in for a rough ride. In short: don't be a jerk, or your jerkosity will be returned to you multi-fold.

When being critiqued, special weight should be given to observations that are logical and irrefutable. If Plot Point A in your story contradicts Plot Point C, if a character in a given profession would never do what you have them doing without shoving in reams of razor-thin justification, or if your terminology or research is incorrect, take the criticism and be thankful because that person just saved you considerable embarrassment in the event of its submission or publication. But if someone says, *I didn't care for this character*, that doesn't necessarily mean you got it wrong, only that *this* person couldn't relate to *that* character or to the role the character plays in the story. That being said, there may be some elements that aren't working but which you can't see because you're too close to the work. So rather than dismissing their concerns out of hand, ask *why* it didn't work for them in case there's anything that can be done to enhance the character's viability without compromising your vision. That way, even if the character ends up right back where you started, you've thought the process through and can defend your choices.

Such workshops, both in and out of academia, can be amazing opportunities for growth. Over time, however, the non-college-based workshops can also become very insular, with self-reinforcing notions of what does and doesn't work. Once you know what the group likes and what they don't, it's easy to begin subconsciously writing toward their sensibilities and preferences. To combat this, the instructor should generate a fair amount of churn when running a workshop, bringing in new voices to shake things up and keep the room from devolving into familiar patterns.

Similarly, attendees of long-term workshops should never stay in the same group for more than a year. After that, you should either find a different workshop where your skills will be challenged in new ways, or withdraw for a while to work on your craft alone, integrating what you learned during those sessions before coming back for an assessment.

Workshops can be as harrowing as they are constructive, validating those who are strong in their work, strengthening those who are still learning their craft, and paring away the weak, the untalented, and the pretentious. That last bit may sound harsh, but it's the only way to keep the workshop focused on those who have demonstrated real skills and have at least a chance to make it as writers.

But what if you're wrong about the "untalented and pretentious"? I hear you cry. And you're right. Many talented writers were written off early only to come roaring back, guns blazing. But there's a qualitative difference between a beginning writer whose work is flawed, and someone who will never, ever hear the music. The hard part is telling them apart, which is an unhappy but necessary step in allocating time and resources to the group as a whole. And sometimes the only way to drill down to the truth is through tough love.

You say you're a writer. I want to believe you, but right now your work doesn't support that. Honestly, it's just not on par with the rest of the class, and I'm not sure this is the right place for you. If you think I have my head up my ass, then prove it. Learn your art. Write better. Write deeper. Show me I'm wrong, because nothing in all of creation would make me happier.

The path to a writing career is incredibly difficult, so if mere criticism can cause someone to turn away, there's no way they would survive the process later, when things get really tough. But someone who has to write, who *needs* to write, cannot be turned aside. For them there is no other choice. Writing is as much a part of them as their DNA. Try all you want to stop them, and they'll just come back stronger, more determined than ever to prove you wrong.

Writing workshops are not nurseries or counseling centers. They are gladiatorial arenas where attendees strap on their armor and fight for their craft and their vision.

So grab your sword and shield and get to it.

SANDING IT DOWN

A quotation of unknown origin and variable phraseology, alternately attributed to Michelangelo, Leonardo Da Vinci, and other famous sculptors, is frequently thrown around by writers and artists as an explication of the creative process: "The sculpture is already complete within the marble block before I begin my work. I just have to chisel away the superfluous material." Another version is, "To sculpt a horse, I start off with a block of marble and simply chisel away everything that isn't a horse."

And while that's as good a description as anything else, it falls short in one crucial respect. Focusing the reader's mind solely on the magnificent marble sculpture diverts our attention from the even *larger* pile of marble that covers the floor in every direction, all the bits and pieces that were chipped away because they weren't part of the horse.

The editing process, by which a writer chips away everything that isn't essential to the story, is the most important part of the process once you've finished telling the story to yourself. Day after day, inch by inch, you pare down the words, straighten out the grammar, and clarify your intentions until the raw material has been transformed into a gleaming, polished story.

This is also the point where a lot of beginning writers get seriously hung up.

Our natural inclination, especially in the early years, is to believe that whatever we've just written is perfect exactly as it is, without alteration or adjustment. That's how it came out of us so that's how it should forever be, frozen in amber for all time. So when someone says, "You know, it's really kind of long," or "I thought the middle was a bit slow," it comes across as a credibility attack on the divinity of our work and we get our backs up, becoming even *more* convinced that the words are sacrosanct and should not, must not, *cannot* be changed.

I can remember, keenly and indelibly, what that felt like.

I was an ass.

Anyone who's ever taken shop class in high school knows that you can't just cut and nail some raw boards together and call it a cabinet. The wood has to be sanded down until smooth, slotted carefully into place and secured, then oiled and stained until it is appealing to the eye and pleasant to the touch. Writing is no different. You want the reader to start at the first line of your story, then slide effortlessly down the prose until they hit the end, sometimes without even realizing how long they've been reading. *I couldn't put it down . . . I started at page one, then didn't look up again until nearly midnight . . . It was smooth as glass . . .* Those are the sort of comments you want the work to elicit.

My approach to editing is quite simple: I start off by saying everything I *can* say about a subject, sand it down to everything I *want* to say about it, then sand it down again to only what I *need* to say.

(To make the point, the preceding paragraph originally began: "When anyone asks me about editing, I tell them that . . ." I deleted the material because it was an unnecessary attempt to justify making a point that didn't require justification.) (And I just edited the end of the preceding sentence, which originally read "any such justification" before I took out *any such* because the intent was implicit.)

I love reading manuscripts that have been hand-revised by the author because that's where you see the mind of the writer at work, chewing through sentences and almost always paring down rather than adding to the material. What a writer takes out of his or her work is often as important as what they leave in. (That was originally "Often, what a writer takes out of his or her work," but that structure inserted an unnecessary clause so I started it with "What" instead and moved "often" further down the sentence; the fewer times you have to break up your work with commas, the more smoothly it will read. Would you, gentle reader, have noticed that extra clause and the pause after the first word? Probably not. But it's obvious now that you know it was there.)

First drafts are buckets into which we dump all the elements of our story, which is why so many firsts are overwritten and heavy on exposition; we want to be sure that the reader understands *exactly* what we're trying to say, so we explain everything in excruciating detail. Not only are the expositional sections lengthy and overdone, we sometimes repeat or restate information we deem important several times, creating unnecessary redundancy. Also, repetition. Not to mention saying the same thing more than once in slightly different ways in the hope that no one will notice.

The preceding paragraph was brought to you by the Department of Redundancy Department.

Paring down the work doesn't mean sacrificing your voice or style. If anything, cutting away the clutter makes both those things more evident, just as eliminating static from a signal makes the voices on the recording clearer and more distinct. (I'd originally concluded this paragraph with an additional sentence, "There's just less in the way," to hammer home the point, but that would be restating the obvious and the reader doesn't deserve to be hit over the head like that.)

And yes, the revision process can be agonizing. I edited this book *five times* before sending it on to the publisher, sanding it down line by line, word by word, comma by comma, each revision more specific than the one before, going over it and over it until all I wanted in the world was to run into the backyard and scream really loud. But since the neighbors would have called the cops, I redirected the impulse into having several large pieces of chocolate. Chocolate is the universal panacea, and don't let anyone tell you otherwise.

When editing your work (that was originally "When sitting down to edit your work" but the action described is unnecessary to the process statement, and besides, who am I to judge your posture?) (*besides* could probably be cut out of the preceding sentence, but if I start editing the edits we'll be here all night, and there has to be *some* imperfection in the work, no?), there are several areas in particular that deserve your attention.

One of the oft-stated rules of editing is that you can usually delete the first paragraph or page of a short story, and the first chapter of a novel, without doing undue violence to the work. I'm not entirely sure this hard-and-fast rule applies in all cases at all times, but there is merit to its intent.

When we start writing something, it sometimes feels as if we have to give ourselves permission to write it, or encouragement for the reader to read it, so the first bits tend to feather around the edges before getting to the point. The same applies to sentence and paragraph construction. "I always thought that growing up in Kanas City was tough," versus just saying it without the preface: "Growing up in Kansas City was tough." Neither you nor your characters need to seek validation or permission before making a statement. If their experience is that growing up in Kansas City was tough, they don't need to lead off by saying it's their opinion because otherwise they wouldn't be saying it.

(One exception to the rule above comes into play when your character is insecure with their opinion and thus tends to speak in conditional sentences, which you consciously include as a way to demonstrate their personality. Absent that, get to the point.)

Once you've cut down the beginning to just the really necessary bits, sift through the rest of your story, keeping in mind the Three Cs: Condense, Combine, and Collapse.

Condense: This is what I've been doing throughout this chapter, sanding down each paragraph and removing extraneous words to focus on the essential point being made.

Combine: One of the surest marks of a neophyte writer is a tendency to write scenes that do only one thing at a time. Character A talks to Character B, gets some vital information, then in the next scene Character A gets a call from Character C regarding some other part of the story. It's linear and sensible but structurally uninteresting. Combining scenes would have Character A trying to get information out of Character B when a call comes in from Character C, which Character B uses as a way to deflect or get out of town. This gives the reader more meat in each scene and provides conflict, which helps exposition go down easier.

Collapse: look for whole scenes or chapters that don't add significantly to the story and take them out completely. If a twenty-page chapter only contains one important bit, take that part out and slide it somewhere else, ditching the rest completely. If it *can* be cut, it *should* be cut. Similarly, if two characters are serving roughly the same role in the story, see if you can collapse them into one character. This results in one unique character rather than two roughly equivalent characters competing for the spotlight and taking up valuable real estate in your story.

Grind all of that down to its most essential form until there's not an inch of unwanted fat anywhere to be found. Take as much time as you need. Better to get the work done right than get it done Tuesday.

Illustrative of that point: For many years before his passing, famed writer and radio dramatist Norman Corwin was a friend of mine. Norman, in turn, had been best pals with Carl Sandburg, arguably one of America's finest poets. They were drawn together by a love of language, and spent many dinners in each other's company, discussing the work. So it was only natural that Norman would invite him to stay for a month in a guest house at his home in Sherman Oaks, California.

"One morning Carl came in for breakfast," Norman said, "and he was searching in his pocket for something, and he couldn't find it, so he emptied his pockets on the coffee table the way you would lay out pocket change. Out came little round balls of paper the texture of dandelion puffs. They'd been in there for so long that they had the consistency of cloth. Some were almost crumbling with age. I noticed there was writing in pencil on some of them, and when I looked closer I found that they contained little slivers of poems. I said, 'May I read some of these?' He said sure.

"They were little gems, all of them, and I said, 'My god, Carl, these are wonderful, how long have you had them?'

"He said, 'Well, some of them are ten years old, others twelve, fourteen maybe.'

"'Why haven't you published them?'

"'I'm not through with them yet,' he said, and slipped them back into his pocket."

The time it takes to get it right, is the time it takes to get it right, no more, no less.

You must always strive to be as objective as possible when editing your work. If necessary, you can pretend it was given to you by someone else, or that it's been slotted to appear in a magazine with limited room, and the only way it will fit requires cutting the word count by 20 percent. Grind it down, then grind it down again. Once you think it's as tight as it'll go, look for ten words per page that can be deleted. You'll find them every time. Then, just as an experiment, do it again, aiming to delete five more words per page.

Once you've reached a point in your editing when you cannot find a single extraneous word, there's still one last pass ahead of you.

We all have a tendency to write the first word that comes to mind, or the almost-right word that sits on the shelf *next* to the right word, because they sound right or we're too caught up in the rush of words to take a dictionary break. But writing is all about precision, about taking care to say exactly what you mean to say, no less, no more.

Does the room smell musty? Or does it smell of old wood and dry paint?

Is your antagonist determined or is he relentless?

Is he *brittle* or is he *frangible*? The meanings are similar, but to be brittle is to be inflexible and easily offended; to be frangible is to be easily cracked or broken. When you use a piece of fresh chalk on a board for the first time, the edges crack off in little bits and pieces. That's frangible, and the difference between the two terms is subtle but telling.

True, some people may not know the word *frangible*, but that's why God made search engines. It's not your problem. Your job, your solemn responsibility, is to always use the word that says most clearly what you intend to say. At risk of dragging French into this, it's the difference between the *bon mot* and the *mot juste*. The *bon mot* is what one frequently sees in popular movies, the funny, clever, or ironic turn of phrase, so we tend to reach for that first, even though it can feel self-aware and forced. The *mot juste*, on the other hand, is the absolutely correct and appropriate word. So, unless you're illustrating a character trait, one should always aspire for the *mot juste*, not the *bon mot*, because finding the single right word will save you from having to drop in several *almost*-right words next to it in an effort to carry the same narrative weight. Be precise in your writing, even and especially when you want it to feel sloppy. The Drunken Fist style of martial arts is designed to replicate the mannerisms of someone who's inebriated, but the precision behind those moves takes years to master. Similarly, making a character sound illiterate or poorly spoken often requires an extreme degree of precision if he is to sound authentic.

When you finally reach the end of the editing process, the story should read like a bullet, lean and muscular and tight. Ideally, the next step is to put it in a drawer for a week, then pull it out for one last read to make sure you didn't take out too much, sacrificing clarity for brevity. The editing process is a constant battle between saying too much and being dull, or saying too little and being obscure.

A writer/director friend of mine had a tendency to write detailed dialogue and exposition in his scripts, making sure everything was clear, only to cut it all out by the time he finished shooting and editing on the theory that "it's all obvious." Well, yes, it was obvious to *him* because he knew what had originally been there, but the audience didn't have the benefit of reading the script, and his movies were rightly pilloried for being confusing, which eventually led him to repent and reconsider his editorial philosophy.

Similarly, whether writing a script or a novel, the story has to be clear to a reader who doesn't have your insight from having written and rewritten it thirty times. If you find any points that need greater clarity, drop in just enough to get the point across and no more.

Then, and only then, are you done with the thing.

But twenty bucks says that if you look at it a year later, you'll find all *kinds* of things you want to revise.

BUILDING CHARACTERS AND WORLDS

During the 1950s, a period many consider the Golden Age of Science Fiction, the general public tended to perceive science fiction as a fairly sterile genre, more about the Big Ideas, the technology, or the plot than the characters. The square-jawed male protagonists were as superficial as asphalt and invariably Caucasian, the female characters were either absent or relegated to secondary importance, and the stories were technical and far from entertaining. There was a brief flurry of more dynamic, character-based stories in the sixties, a trend known as New Wave Science Fiction, but the troublemakers were soon expelled from the Temple of SF, allowing the genre to fall back into a sleepy and rather stiff mode of storytelling that for the most part persists to this day, which is why there are few print SF fandoms that can rival the appeal of such fantasy titles as the Harry Potter novels.[1]

As a young writer making his first forays into the genre, my stories also tended to be about the Big Ideas, the technology, or the plot because I thought that's what writing *was*. This resulted in stories that were hopelessly malformed and wretched beyond description. It took years for me to understand that regardless of genre or medium, the audience is there for

---

1 It's only been in (very) recent years that science fiction has begun to experience a bit of a cultural revolution, with more diverse writers and characters breaking through the barricades to tell stories for a new and equally diverse readership.

the *characters*, not the technical gimmick or the cool idea. They are the ones we root for (or against) and what we remember the most of what we read.

You may not remember every detail of the whaling technology described at great length in *Moby Dick*, but you remember Ishmael, Queequeg, and Ahab.

You may not know everything about the German occupation of France in *Casablanca*, but you remember Rick, Ilsa, and Signor Ferrari.

The specifics of the police corruption behind the New York's Finest "taxi service" in *The Usual Suspects* may get lost over time, but you remember Kobayashi, Dean Keaton, and Keyser Söze.

At its core, all writing is about character. The circumstances may be compelling, the stakes vast, the music stirring, and the special effects dazzling to the eye . . . but if there isn't a strong, compelling character at the center of it, someone the audience wants to spend time with, all that's left is what Shakespeare described as "a tale told by an idiot, full of sound and fury, signifying nothing." They must be compelling on their own terms and involved with the other characters in dynamic, interesting relationships, because those connections ground them *and* us, giving the story dramatic or personal stakes to push against.

A few years ago, I worked with James Cameron (*Titanic, Terminator, Avatar*) on a project for Warner Bros. Jim is five steps beyond brilliant, which made the collaboration both a great experience and extremely educational. During one of our sessions, he said, "You know, I used to think that writing science fiction was all about writing familiar characters in unfamiliar settings. It took me twenty years to realize I was wrong. It's about familiar *relationships* in unfamiliar settings." Recognizable relationships are the gateway drug to the rest of the story. So *Terminator 2* is a father-son story, even though it's not, just as *Aliens* is a mother-daughter story, even though it's not. A reader or audience member may not be able to buy into the idea of robots from the future or starships or aliens, but they can definitely buy into those relationships, and once they're invested, a good chunk of your job as a storyteller is done.

So when I worked on the first *Thor* movie from Marvel Studios, I felt strongly that as much fun as it would be to see the fights, the special effects, and Asgard made manifest, in the end the movie had to be about two sons competing for their father's affection. *That*, not the cool visuals, was the gravitational center of the story.

During a later meeting with director Sir Kenneth Branagh on the set of *Thor*, where I was to appear in a cameo (he was great but I was awful; I have no business being in front of a camera, anywhere, ever, for any reason), he said that having come out of Shakespearean theater and film, the competitive relationship between Thor and Loki was essential to his understanding of the story and a key factor behind his decision to direct the movie.

The path from *my work is wretched beyond description* to *holy crap, Sir Kenneth thinks I'm cool* runs straight through characterization. Character isn't a consequence of plot, character *is* plot; the more you know about your characters, the more organic the storytelling process becomes because they can help you figure things out from inside the story.

Here's the corollary: Picture your best friend walking across the living room at night, the lights off. Suddenly he or she bangs their shin hard on the coffee table. Now, you know your friend, so you know exactly what they will say when this happens and how they will say it. You don't have to work at it or struggle, you just know. Writing is no different. You get to know your characters so well that whatever situation you drop them into, you can just sit back and write down what they do in response.

Once you've fully fleshed out your characters, the writing process becomes weirdly collaborative, almost Zen-like, as you surrender yourself to the flow of what happens next. The best way to conceptualize that is to imagine an old-fashioned ballroom playing a waltz: at one end of the room is a guy who just got out of the Arthur Murray Dance School, and he's doing fine, but you can see him in his head going *one-two-three, one-two-three*. At the other end of the room is Fred Astaire . . . and he's just dancing.

There's *trying* to dance, and there's *dancing*.

There's *trying* to write, and there's *writing*.

And the first part of surrendering to that inner music comes out of character.

Interesting characters are more readily created by working from the inside-out, by figuring out who they are, than by working from the outside-in, which is more about what they do and the role they play in the jigsaw puzzle that is the plot, especially when it comes to writing procedural stories. The best way to develop those strong characters from the inside-out is to ask the next logical question, fundamental interrogatories that will provide most of the fuel needed to tell your story: Who is your character, what does s/he want to achieve, how far will they go to accomplish it, and how far will someone else go to stop them, and why?

Let's start with *who*.

Plant a flower, then pour red dye on the ground, and as it grows a red circle will appear in the stem. We are all the product of the soil we grew in, so the first logical question is, where does the character come from? (Let's call him Tyler just so I can avoid having to type *the character* ten thousand times in the next few pages.) You can't just say *the East Coast* because that covers everything from the tip of Florida to the Canadian border. Pick a place and be specific. Creating a compelling character requires paying attention to the tiniest, most intimate details.

Okay, he's from New York.

Not good enough. Someone reared in Manhattan will come out very different from someone who calls the Bronx his home.

Fine, Midtown.

Nope. Still not there. Where in Midtown?

Are you freaking kidding me?

Do I look like I'm kidding you?

Show me what you look like when you're kidding and I'll let you know.

Get serious. Pick a place.

Okay, so . . . how about he grew up around 29th Street and 8th Avenue?

Interesting.

Why is that interesting?

Well, if New York is a melting pot, the spot you chose is the center of community-based multiculturalism in the Manhattan area. You're within walking distance of Koreatown, which is a safe place of transition for many Koreans and Chinese immigrants who have recently arrived in the United States. The Garment District and the Diamond District are just up the street, so he's going to be running into Orthodox and Reformed Jews as well as Israelis, along with their clients from the worlds of fashion and business. And just to the east is Little Brazil. So rather than running into individual immigrants spread throughout a given part of town, Tyler would grow up immersed in supportive, multicultural *communities*, familial environments that feel different from some of the other parts of Manhattan because they're more culturally cohesive.

So he might have a broader outlook on other countries than somebody from the Bronx.

He could. This level of exposure isn't a requirement for being open-minded, but it doesn't hurt. And since he'd be walking into areas with a lot of non-English speakers, he'd probably have to pick up some of the local language just as a matter of enlightened self-interest... smatterings of Hebrew, Yiddish, Joseon-mal—

What's that?

Korean and Mandarin. Do they not have Google where you are? And here's something else: if he goes west instead of east, he runs into Chelsea, a very upscale, hip, and expensive neighborhood. Big money.

Wow, with a range like that . . . turn left and you're in one world, turn right you're in another . . . he'd probably never be sure where he really belonged or fit in.

You're starting to get it. Now here's the clincher: the intersection you gave me is not far from the Hudson River piers and shipping areas, the kind of places he'd trek to as a kid to sit and watch the big ships coming and going from all around the world.

Yeah . . .

So, who's your character?

He's a guy who had to learn fast how to fit in, even if that meant faking it. As a survival mechanism he picked up bits of at least four languages while growing up so if he got in trouble or got lost he'd be able to ask for help. On one side he sees people with tons of money being all self-involved with their status and cars and a lot of them probably not giving a rat's ass about anyone else, and on the other side are people with little money but big dreams who look after and support each other. Being able to see the good and bad of both sides means he probably doesn't feel like he belongs to either one of them. He's restless, smart—

How do you know he's smart?

How many languages can you *speak, pal?*

Point taken.

He's gonna want to explore the world, to find out where those ships go and what's at the other end. Growing up around those self-supporting communities would probably teach him about the importance of family and people helping each other, so maybe that's something he'd want to do. Not as a cop necessarily, too obvious, but maybe in finance, or a translator, or maybe he wants to work for the State Department . . . hey, turns out the UN is right around the corner. Maybe he goes to college, interns at the UN, and learns about international relations. Could even end up CIA, perfect job for a guy who feels like he doesn't fit in anywhere and wants to travel the world. A job that would help him figure out who he is.

Back up a little. Remember, we're trying to keep this rooted in character development. Is there a person or incident in his youth that you think would set him firmly on the path of looking after people? Someone who can also be important in his present life?

I see him as a thirteen-year-old in Little Brazil, just out of school for the day, and he's all by himself and three guys try to brace him for whatever money he's got, but an old guy comes out of a restaurant and stands between them, big guy, like one of those Easter Island megaliths, and stares them down, or maybe one of them tries something and he puts the guy down hard, right in the middle of the street.

How would this affect Tyler?

Well, he'd be grateful for sure, maybe offer the guy the money the thugs wanted to steal—which the guy won't take, of course—but it's an honorable thing to do and the old guy doesn't see that a lot, and he appreciates the gesture. So he takes Tyler under his wing, like a mentor, talks to him about the place he came from, why he left, what he hopes to do in America. Has a huge impact on his future.

The red ring around the stem of a flower.

A little corny, but yeah, exactly.

Is there anything else that could further connect them or provide a story arena?

Well, I just did the Google thing, and guess what? Turns out there are a ton of diamond mines in Brazil, so the old guy would probably have some connections over in the Diamond District.

Okay. So now you have *two* characters where, a second ago, you didn't have any. Asking who Tyler is and where he comes from led you to his job and a friendship with a Brazilian expatriate who probably has connections to guys in the Diamond District. If you go with Tyler working for the CIA or the State Department, how would all of that tie together in a story?

Maybe the old guy calls him one day, as scared as Tyler was the day those guys tried to ambush him, saying he's in trouble and needs help. But by the time he gets there, the guy's been murdered and there are diamonds in his pocket, too many to have gotten legally.

And how would Tyler feel about that?

He'd definitely want to investigate his friend's murder.

Was the Brazilian in the country legally or illegally?

Hard to say, but I'm guessing he might have come in over the border on his own.

So how would the State Department or the CIA feel about him digging into a case involving someone who came to the US illegally?

They'd be against it.

So they'd be antagonists, right alongside whoever killed Tyler's friend.

Yeah.

Would that stop him?

Hell no. This guy was like a father. He'd do it anyway.

So your story is about a government employee whose friend is murdered, and he's determined to find out why. So against the recommendation of his bosses he dives into the world of high finance and the international diamond trade in an investigation that stretches from New York to Brazil and potentially other countries as well. And not only does he have the Bad Guys to worry about, his own people are trying to stop him. There are a lot of ways he could end up being fired, hurt, or killed, but he keeps chasing the case anyway, not because somebody ordered him to do it, which is okay but not very interesting, but because he cared about his friend and this is personal to him. The story comes directly out of his character, and his character is central to the story.

Yeah, that's right, and hey, both characters grew from the inside-out! How about that?

You now know who your main character is, what he wants, how far he's prepared to go, and the first indications of how far others will go to stop him. You even have some ideas for relationship scenes and action pieces that can help jump-start the writing process. But the *best* thing is that this entire process began by just making a decision and picking a street corner. From there you were able to map out what kind of environments he would have been exposed to while growing up, determine how this would affect him as an adult, and where it would lead him, simply by asking the next logical question. Now imagine how many more stories, and how varied they can be, when you go from just a street corner to fold in the rest of the world.

That was a segue, wasn't it?

Yep.

Okay, then I guess you better get outta here.

Me?

I only made you up for purposes of this conversation.

No, *I* made *you* up for this conversation.

Wow, no ego on your side, is there? What color is the sky in the world where you live?

Blue.

I . . . wait. Seriously?

Yeah, why? What's the color of the sky where *you* are?

Orange. With rings. Maybe we should talk later.

Sure thing.

It's worth remembering that the characters in your stories are not just people with lines of dialogue. The worlds they occupy are also characters, especially when writing fantasy, horror, or SF, and need to be built from the inside-out with the same degree of precision and consistency as the human characters, using the same next-logical-question methodology.

Let's start with a planet that is featureless and empty, a blank canvas for our endeavor. Is it hot or cold? Let's say hot. Arid or humid? Let's go for arid. So now the world becomes ruddy in appearance, dotted by small seas and just enough patches of green to sustain life. What kind of dominant life-form would evolve in a place like that? They'd have to be physically strong, with hard, thick skin that would let them withstand the withering heat and go without water for extended periods. Since newborns would be vulnerable to these harsh conditions, evolutionary selection might lean toward marsupials or other pouch-based biologies that would enable mothers (and maybe even fathers, why not?) to protect their offspring for as long as possible. They might choose to live beneath the ground, or in flat structures made with rocky, stone-like materials, which would be cooler and allow greater access to moisture.

With so few resources, their history would likely be one of constant warfare over water and arable land. This suggests that warriors and those with a grasp of life-sustaining technology would be highly valued, but there would probably be a religious component as well that could help keep them going through periods of war and extended drought. Water rituals would almost certainly feature prominently in such a belief system. Everyone would be trained from infancy to use weapons, and blades would be a favorite because they don't require fuel or reloading. Frequent wars would lead to the development of governments more akin to feudal states than anything like a republic.

Given the preceding, what can we infer about their manner of dress? In a dry and difficult climate, they would likely prefer leather or other skin-like fabrics that could survive the difficult climate better than cloth, and they would probably be sleeveless and short to avoid generating unwanted additional heat.

Thinking it through in this way gives consistency to every aspect of the world you are creating. The clothes go with the biology; the locations are consistent with the clothes; the political system is consistent with their history; the types of weapons match the kind of society that would emerge; and the belief system makes sense. Done properly, the moment your audience or reader sees even a glimpse of that world or its characters, they will know exactly where they are and who they're looking at.

(And for those familiar with *Babylon 5*, that's *exactly* the series of questions that guided the creation of the Narn homeworld and its occupants.)

The way in which settings are developed and experienced must be consistent and feel real, not just when dealing with alien empires but with our own world as well. If your story is set in a town in Nairobi in the dead of summer, readers should always feel that oppressive heat, even when not directly referenced: mentions of condensation on glasses of cold beer, sweat trickling down the back, dogs too tired to move. You don't have to point to it to point to it, but you do have to keep those textures alive just as you keep your characters alive and in motion.

As the saying goes, "God is in the details," and those fine points only emerge after prolonged research and mindful consideration. Prior to beginning work on *Sense8* for Netflix, the other producer/writers and I did copious amounts of research on the locations we'd chosen—San Francisco, Chicago, Mexico City, London, Berlin, Iceland, Mumbai, Nairobi, and Seoul—then traveled to as many of them as possible to root theoretical research in on-the-ground experience. As Mark Twain once wrote, "A man learns things picking up a cat by the tail that he can learn no other way." There are some things you only learn through firsthand experience. So we visited genetic research facilities in Iceland, toured underground clubs in London, and met with a restaurateur in Mumbai to learn how their business worked from the inside. During our expedition to the corrugated metal shacks in the slums outside Mumbai to study the horrific living conditions endured by so many, fellow executive producer Lana Wachowski pulled me aside.

"Everywhere we go here," she said, "everyone has a big-screen TV even when there isn't a real bed."

"Well, yeah," I said. "Because the bed keeps you in but the TV takes you out."

A few days later, when she turned in her pages for the next chunk of script we were writing, that line was in the dialogue.

Again: It's all about the details.

When a reader picks up your short story or novel, or an executive reads your script, they should feel as though they are actually *in* that place, hanging out with people they find interesting, well rounded, and *real*. If you can offer an experience that feels that genuine, that *authentic*, your work will always stand out against other writers at comparable levels of their careers.

Which brings me to what may be the most important piece of information this book can provide. If you take away nothing else from these chapters, this alone will sustain you.

Beginning writers have a tendency to worry about all the other writers out there trying to break in. They worry about the *competition*.

Here's the secret: the competition . . . isn't.

As someone who has worked with dozens of writers as a producer in TV and in print as an editor, who has taught workshops and judged writing competitions, I can say without equivocation that 90 percent of what's out there at the beginning level is just awful. I'm not saying that the writers lack talent, it's just that you can't tell one way or the other because so many of them fail to do the work needed to focus that talent into something viable. They do only the minimum work necessary to get their idea down on paper, then fire it off in the hope that it will electrify the world. It's only with time and rejection that they begin to understand the necessity of going the extra distance.

If you're prepared to do the work of focusing in on your craft from the beginning, you will be light-years ahead of any so-called "competition." A manuscript written with a professional level of attention to detail, that shows you've put real effort into your characters and your world, your art and your craft, glows in the dark.

You are not competing with other writers.

You are only, and always, competing with yourself.

MUSE-INGS

The image many people associate with writers has roots that go all the way back to the eighteenth century, courtesy of British writers such as John Keats, Lord Byron, and Shelley (Percy and Mary). Readers imagine the author draped across a fainting couch, back of one hand pressed to the forehead, the other hand clutching pen and paper, tortured eyes staring up at the ceiling as they await the arrival of the elusive Muse. This breathless, tortured stereotype was further reinforced by such writers as Edgar Allan Poe, George Bernard Shaw, Victor Hugo, Arthur Rimbaud, and Samuel Taylor Coleridge.

And yes, from time to time every writer longs for a fainting couch as they gaze up at the ceiling and wonder where the hell the words went. But anyone who wants to be a working writer and spends his or her time waiting around for the Muse to strike is betting on the wrong Greek goddess.

In a later chapter, we will discuss the necessity of making time to write. But before we can even get to setting schedules, there has to be a mental discipline. If all one wants is to create the occasional poem with months or years in between, then yes, by all means, await the Muse. But that doesn't work if your goal is to make a career as a writer. When an editor, publisher, or producer gives you an assignment with a deadline, they expect you to hit that date. To miss it completely and say, "Well, nothing struck me," is to invite being struck in an entirely different and novel fashion.

The inclination to await the Muse often springs from our assumption that whatever she dictates will be perfect, unlike what we might end up scribbling onto the page. But as noted, the purpose of a first draft is not to be perfect; the goal is to assemble piles of words in something that resembles the right order that can subsequently be revised and improved upon. So force yourself to at least write the first sentence. Yes, it may be terrible, but terrible can be fixed. The void is beyond repair or review. If you can get one sentence on the page, just that much effort will usually trigger another sentence to follow it. If it doesn't, don't leave the desk. Stay there until you've run through the time you've allocated for your work. If nothing else, anger and boredom will force you to begin writing more.

It doesn't need to be flawless; it just needs to *be*.

If after that first sentence you're still stuck and unable to move forward on the story you want to tell, it's okay to segue *briefly* into writing about something else as a writing exercise. Prime the pump by writing about your day, or what you plan to do that evening, or a memory that came to mind about the first time you saw the ocean. Then flip back to what you came here to write. The goal is to get past the inertia of that day's first written words. Writing leads to writing.

Doing this consistently will help you to develop a writing muscle, just as if you were working out at the gym. It hurts at first, but gradually you find yourself experiencing an adrenaline rush every time you sit at the desk, the creative equivalent of endorphins that come from being able to say, *I did this yesterday even when I didn't want to and something good came of it, so I can do it today and maybe even carry a little more of the story than I did previously.* The more you do it, the more you *want* to do it, and like exercise, for some people the process becomes addicting in all the right ways.

When you're ready to stop for the day, *don't finish the last sentence you're writing.* Get to the midpoint of the sentence and stop. This will be a huge help to overcoming the next day's first-sentence inertia, because you already know how that sentence is supposed to end. Most likely it's been spinning around all night, waiting impatiently for you to get in there and finish it. So, when you start writing again, those words go onto the page quickly, seamlessly setting you up for the next sentence.

The key, really, is to find ways to fox yourself into approaching the work relaxed and calm, rather than tensing up, a lesson with all kinds of real-world implications. A few years ago, I hired a professional photographer to come to my home and shoot headshots for my second novel because I was tired of taking my own photos, which upon publication frequently led to visits by law enforcement. There are people the camera loves, people the camera hates, and people who make the camera lock itself in the bathroom crying and refuse to come out all night, and I am very much in the last category.

She spent the first hour unsuccessfully trying to get me to relax. "Just be yourself," she said repeatedly, but since I've never really known who that is, I kept trying to look dignified and serious as I sat at my desk in my very writerly black leather jacket and black shirt. *Posing* rather than *being*. And every time the shutter clicked, the walls came down behind my eyes.

Finally, she threw up her hands in frustration and headed for the door. "Wait here," she said. I wanted to point out that this was my home and I had no plans to leave, but I'd seen the expression in her eyes and didn't want to court catastrophe.

She returned a few moments later with a stack of children's blocks and toys from her car. "I want you to play with these," she said, and dumped them onto the carpet.

I looked at her, then down at the toys, and back at her again. "You want me to get down on the floor?"

"Yes."

"And play with . . . *blocks*."

"And the toys, yes."

"You know I'm an important writer, right?"

Her eyes narrowed. "Get. On. The fuh-*loor*."

I got on the fuh-*loor*.

She lowered herself onto the carpet on the other side of the room and crossed her legs, the camera in her lap. "Now play."

This is stupid, I wanted to say, but my highly tuned instinct for self-preservation dictated otherwise, so I reluctantly started playing with the toys.

I assumed she'd start snapping photos at once, but instead she just sat very still, watching as I used the blocks to spell out profanities only visible on my side of the wall of letters. Then, chin resting on one hand, I turned my attention to the dinosaurs and the cars, and now the dinosaurs were driving cars into the block-walls because they didn't care for the profanities and there were accidents everywhere so I looked around for something that could substitute for an ambulance and—

"Joe!" she said.

I glanced up.

Click!

I straightened, having almost forgotten she was there. "Are we starting now?" I asked.

"Nope, that's the shot," she said. "It's the only unguarded moment you've had since I walked in here, the only time when I could see inside your eyes because you weren't thinking about how you looked or how you were sitting, and you were just being yourself."

And with that, as the saying goes, she packed up her toys and went home.

I don't know if the photo that came out of that experience is the *best* picture anyone's ever taken of me, but I do know that it's the most *authentic*. Because it's the only photo where I was *being in* the moment rather than *thinking about* the moment.

And that is *exactly* how the writing impulse works.

Claims to divinity notwithstanding, the Muse is nothing more than the small, soft voice at the back of your head that tells you what to write and how to write it. It *wants* to help, to come out and play, but if it gets drowned out by the crash and clatter of the conscious mind—which is what happens most of the time—it retreats to sit in the corner and sulk. It can't function, and you can't be what you need to be in that moment if you're stressed out, tense, or overwrought. Rather than succumb to the fear of the first draft, you should feel free to try different things, to experiment or to be silly if that's what it takes to create an environment where your inner Muse can safely come out and play.

Sometimes you have to *distract* yourself *from* yourself to *be* yourself.

Writers who understand this will often look for ways to silence the conscious mind enough to allow the creative impulse to peek out. At one end of the spectrum, these methods include drugs or alcohol, which is why so many creative people have problems with substance abuse. Others meditate, play music, go for a walk in the park, or pull comic book action figures down off the shelf, allegedly for purposes of dusting, but in reality hoping that nostalgia will pop the conscious mind into a warm, fuzzy neutral gear while the subconscious figures out what it wants to say.

And there's much to be said for such grazing. The creativity that lurks within you is like water in a tank, and from time to time that tank has to be refilled or you're going to start having problems. The best way to refill the tank is to give yourself permission to indulge in art and music and beauty. Read books by skilled writers that you think will teach you new ways to use words and inspire you to greatness, but also read just for fun. The more you read, the better you will write. Whenever I hit a bump in the writing process, if I can't find something fun to read, I'll fire up my music library, which is deliberately wide ranging, because you never know what will light up the right neurons with inspiration. There's country and hip-hop and electro swing and rock and classical and jazz and pop and Mongolian metal and folk and death metal and house and trance and dance and even some K-Pop, five thousand tracks covering every genre and form of music ever composed. Sooner or later, the music carries me through to the other side of whatever is bugging me about what I'm writing.

As much as we take from the creative impulse, the proper care and feeding of the Muse requires that we give back in equal measure. In *Treasure of the Sierra Madre*, after Humphrey Bogart and the other characters finish taking the gold from the deep gouts they have torn in a mountain, they are about to head off when Walter Huston's character stops them. "We have to put the mountain back," he tells them. It gave up its riches for them, and the respectful thing now is to put it back the way it was.

Despite their doubts, the others help him to fix the damage they've done.

Your inner Muse gives you the gold, but in return, every so often, you have to put the mountain back.

Another method of getting around the noise of the conscious mind involves striking while it's out of the picture. Again, the subconscious *wants* to help you tell stories, and since the only time it reigns supreme is when we're asleep, you can use that window to your advantage.

When you're in bed, in that twilight stage between wakefulness and sleep, load up whatever story problem has been plaguing you recently. Not all of them, just the one that has been the most resistant to solution. Don't try and solve it right then, because it won't work and you'll never get any sleep. Just gently load up the structure and your questions, so it's all there but your conscious mind isn't yelling about it, then let yourself fall asleep.

As soon as you're zonked out, the subconscious will leap on that problem like a cat with a string because now it has something *fun* to do, something creative and constructive. In most cases it'll stay on that problem all night until it finally breaks through to an answer.

When you awake the next morning, while you're still in that midway stage, gently poke around your mind to see what gifts the Muse may have left for you while you were asleep. Most times there will be at least *some* kind of solution waiting for you, as long as you don't come at it too loudly or aggressively upon awaking and scare it off.

It's easy for writers to attribute what we do to something outside ourselves, because no one *really* knows where stories come from. So we call it the Muse and wait for it to show up and save us from ourselves. But the Muse is us and we are the Muse. We just have to see that writing is as much play as discipline and be willing to get out of our own way so that our bespoke inner Muse can whisper stories to us in the dark without being censored, controlled, or doubted. The more we can become as clear as glass, allowing the words and the creative impulse to flow through us uninterrupted and unfiltered, the more the writing will improve.

It's a difficult dance to dance, because we are logical creatures and sometimes it's hard to find the balance between the rigor the conscious mind demands and the creative chaos the subconscious enjoys.

Oscar Wilde wrote:

Love will die if held too tightly
Love will fly if held too lightly
Lightly, tightly, how do I know
Whether I'm holding or letting love go?

Clutch the Muse too tightly, sublimating the creative spark to the need for control, and you'll strangle it. Treat it without respect or regard, and it will simply fly off, because no one should stay in a relationship where they are not being appreciated.

But once you can strike a balance between waiting around endlessly for the Muse to show up and banging on its door, wonderful things begin to happen very quickly.

YOU CAN'T SELL AN IDEA

The emails come almost daily. *I've got this great idea for a movie/TV series/ novel/short story, would you like to buy it, or tell me how I can sell it to a studio/ network/publisher . . . if I give you my idea and you write it we can split the money 50/50 . . .* and one more literally from this morning, *I'm looking for someone who can work with me to package my ideas and sell them, can you help me?*

No.

Because nobody wants your ideas.

(And I don't know what *package my ideas* even means. Put them in a box? Staple them together? *Here's a six-pack of ideas, want 'em? They also come in twelve and sixteen packs of double-ply ideas in decorator patterns that won't clog the pipes.*)

Unless you've figured out a Unified Field Theory or faster-than-light travel (in which case yeah, contact me and we'll split the money 50/50), ideas are worthless, a dime a dozen. Give ten writers the same basic idea and you'll get back eleven stories. What matters is the execution of that idea (rather than its assassination), which is entirely a function of the person writing it.

Consider the idea of U.S. Air Force bombers overshooting their fail-safe point during the Cold War and, despite every effort to recall them, dropping their payloads and triggering a nuclear holocaust. One version of that idea gave us the somber, relentless character drama *Fail Safe*, starring Henry Fonda. Another version, released the same year, was *Dr. Strangelove or: How I Learned to Stop Worrying and Love the Bomb*, which starred Peter Sellers and ranks as one of the best dark comedies ever committed to film.

They're the same premise, the same idea (so much so that there was much legal wrangling between the studios involved), but they could not possibly be more different.

Talent is the product of training and natural inclination focused through a unique point of view, implemented with an insane degree of dedication and the determination to strive for a level of achievement sufficient to set them apart from the crowd and lift them out of the ordinary.[1] Lots of people can sing. Nina Simone is a one-off. Paul Simon is a one-off. Aretha Franklin is a one-off. Frank Sinatra is a one-off. Janis Joplin is a one-off. They could take songs you've heard a thousand times and, through their interpretation, make you hear them in ways you'd never even *thought* about before.

Writers are performers no less than singers; we're just quieter. Whatever success we achieve is the direct result of how we interpret the story we wish to tell, and how well we are able to communicate that interpretation to someone else. Ideas are just the *start* of that process, they are not the process *in toto*. Let's say you have the most amazing idea in the history of amazing ideas. What's a studio or publisher to do with it? They can't publish it as is, or build a film shoot around it. Can you imagine tuning in to a TV network one evening and someone on-screen says, "We had this guy come to us yesterday with an amazing idea, check this out," and he reads you something covering about half a page? Ideas are useless on their own terms; even if someone were to buy your idea (which they won't because no one does), they'd *still* have to give the idea to another writer who could actually render that into something practicable, and whose interpretation would be so vastly different from your own that it's no longer even the same idea, so why do they need *you*?

As much as we like to think we've come up with an idea no one's thought of before, the odds are pretty good that whatever we've stumbled upon has been encountered by other writers over the long course of human history. That should not be taken to mean that there is nothing new under the sun, or that all art is just reinterpretation of what went

1 This is similar to the ancient Greek definition of happiness: "The exercise of vital powers, along lines of excellence, in a life affording them scope."

before, justifications that are often used for plagiarism and excessive sampling. *It wasn't new when the other guy wrote it, so I'm entitled to take it and use it however I want.* There is a profound difference between an idea, which can be, and in many cases is, generic or broadly thematic, and the expression of that idea in ways that are unique to the artist and specific to the time and culture in which it is created. (For more on this, see the chapter on writer's block.)

It's the *interpretation* of an idea that makes it feel fresh; by the time it comes out the other end of the crazy-straw of your particular talent as a finished work, it looks like nothing that's been done before because *you* haven't been here before.

Absent that interpretation into finished form, story ideas are not just unwanted by most writers, they're potentially dangerous, especially when unsolicited. Writers have ended up in costly legal battles because something they wrote in their own universe bore some resemblance to online fan fiction, or a suggestion posted to a forum where the writer was known to hang out. This has led many writers to adopt a zero-tolerance policy when it comes to fans posting ideas or linking to stories online. For my part, I ask only that if someone is going to write something in one of my fictional universes that they keep it away from any forum where I might stumble upon it. But despite having requested since the Early Cretaceous Period that folks online abide by my "No Story Ideas" rule, some people still continue to post their ideas or stories on the mistaken assumption that they're being helpful (they're not), that it will help their career (it won't), or because they're straight-up pathological.

I was pursued online for *years* by a guy who said he had an idea for the perfect ending for a series I'd produced that never went past the first season. Even though there was no way he could have the right ending because the information needed to reach it would only have been brought out during the intervening seasons, he was adamant about getting me to read his ideas. He came at me on Facebook. I blocked him without looking at his material. He created a new account. I blocked him again. He got my email and came at me directly. I blocked him. He changed email addresses, and when my assistant intercepted his next volley, he became abusive with her.

Another individual popped up online saying that he had written a story set in one of my fictional universes and wanted me to read and give it my stamp of approval for his own personal satisfaction. Once again, I said no and blocked him. In response, he switched up accounts and came at me again. Over and over.

I've never read either of these pieces and will *never* read them, because I don't like being stalked and bullied, and because I have the right to say no. (I suspect that guys like this, and they're *always* guys, have problems with being told "no" that extend far beyond TV writers.)

And the thing is, *this sort of thing has been happening for as long as I've been working in television.* Somebody will come at me with ideas or stories set in worlds I've created, demanding I read them. Some can be discouraged, but others simply don't get the message. On three occasions the stalking—online and, in one case, in person at conventions—became so virulent that I had to enlist the services of private investigators to find them. Usually it only takes making their family members (or in one circumstance, the stalker's employer, since he was using the office computer for purposes of harassment) aware of what's going on to trigger an intervention and make it stop. But that doesn't make the months and dollars spent, and the emotional turmoil endured, any easier.

That being said, in most cases, the danger of unwanted story ideas can be dealt with sensibly. While I was producing *Babylon 5*, a fan posted a story idea on a forum where I was known to hang out that was similar to a script I'd recently finished writing for the series. Since having access to his idea provided grounds that could trigger a lawsuit, the script was removed from the shooting schedule until I could track down the individual and get him to sign a release form acknowledging the situation. Had I not taken such measures, the studio would have scuttled the script, just to be safe. If this seems extreme, I commend the reader to research the number of times when ideas or fan fiction set within the universe of a given writer ended up in court when the ideas proved too similar.

Other than vivisection, sending a writer an unsolicited story idea is honestly one of the rudest and most infuriating things one can do. This is why my assistant screens my physical mail. If she finds a story idea in the pile she re-seals the envelope and sends it back with the notation UNREAD

BY JMS, NEVER DO THIS AGAIN written in bright red ink. It doesn't matter if the other person says, "I'll give it to you free, I'll sign a release form," it's maddening so just don't do it, okay?

Writers spend their lives building careers and reputations because doing so gives us the leverage and freedom to tell stories that are personally resonant and important to us, *not* so that we can tell your stories. We don't need some stranger's ideas, we don't want to risk being sued, and harassment is not the appropriate response to either of those preceding clauses.

Returning to the point about selling one's ideas instead of giving them away or posting them, whenever I conduct a writing workshop there's always at least one person who approaches me afterward to say that despite having no prior experience writing TV scripts, they've spent the last six months writing a pilot for a new series and do I have any advice as to how they can get it sold?

Though it pains me deeply, I have to tell them a very hard thing: that they spent those six months writing something they cannot and will not sell. Naturally, they don't want to hear it and try to cite prior examples of people selling pilots without prior TV credits, but those stories are like unicorns, rumored and reported but never actually seen in the wild. The examples evaporate in the harsh light of web searches confirming that the person in question was either an established writer's offspring or had at least *some* prior experience writing for TV.

An unproduced, inexperienced writer cannot sell a pilot. It just never happens.

Here's why.

As noted, story ideas have no value because it all comes down to how that idea is expressed. The same applies to television, with the added caveat that whoever writes the pilot is generally the same person who goes on to run the show, and before handing over that kind of authority, the networks and studios want to understand your process as a storyteller and have a comfort factor with your experience as a producer. The only way to get that experience is to come up the ranks from freelance writer to staff writer to story editor, then on to co-producer, producer, and eventually executive producer, until you've finally acquired the clout needed to run your own show, and the networks have some idea of your approach to storytelling.

If that seems unfair or closed-minded, let me turn the question around: If you were boarding a flight from New York to Melbourne, who would you prefer to have at the controls: a pilot who has logged hundreds of hours of flight time on this route, or the guy who plans to start attending flight school next Thursday? The queasy feeling you just got in the pit of your stomach is exactly why there's not a TV network or streamer on the planet that will hand you millions of dollars to make a series unless they're absolutely confident that you won't drive the car off the road halfway through shooting. It's about trust as much as what's on the page.

And the prospect of convincing a working writer/producer who *does* have the chops to sell a series to collaborate with you is extremely unlikely (unless that person is already a friend, but that situation can get very awkward very fast). The gift of being allowed to create a new TV series is hard won, extremely remunerative, and can be easily torpedoed if something goes wrong. If a writer/producer can sell shows on his/her own, why would they bring in a project by an unknown writer, for whom they'll have to fight like hell to get network approval (which likely won't come), *and* sacrifice 50 percent of what they'd normally earn for one of their own series, with absolutely no guarantee that you won't blow up the entire process through inexperience?

Answer: they wouldn't.

And they don't.

Which is why it hasn't happened, isn't happening, and isn't *going* to happen.

If you want to sell a TV series, start by writing for established shows and work your way up. Focus on stories that let you demonstrate your unique perspective, and take the time to learn your craft on the writing and producing sides. Gradually, as you move up the ranks, the networks and studios will get comfortable with you and your creative process. Only then will you have the opportunity to sell a pilot and run your own series.

Again, it's not about *ideas*. Ideas that lack interpretation, effort, and the willingness to put them into workable form are the currency of people with short attention spans and no discernible ability. It's about stories, about what that idea means to you and where you want to take it, followed by all the hard work needed to transform that idea into a script or a novel or a short story.

That being said: If you've worked out the whole faster-than-light travel thing, seriously, call me.

SHARK ALERT!

I n preparing to write this volume, I scoped out other writing-related books to see what topics were discussed and, perhaps more to the point, what subjects were *not* covered. Many of these books were quite good, most were middle-of-the-road, and a few brought to mind a review by Dorothy Parker, in which she stated, "This is not a novel to be tossed aside lightly. It should be thrown with great force."

As I continued researching, I was astonished to learn that none of these books had anything to say about those who prey, consciously or otherwise, on beginning writers. But it is an absolutely vital subject because it happens so frequently, and so easily, to so many; the only reason this chapter appears halfway through *Becoming a Writer* is that I didn't want to scare off readers prematurely.

Irving Thalberg, who created and ran MGM, once famously said, "Writers are the most important people in Hollywood, but we must never tell the sons of bitches." Without scripts, without words on a page, directors, actors, and wardrobe designers have nothing to work with. The same applies to other venues; without the written word, book publishers, magazines, blogs, and game designers have nothing to do and would swiftly go out of business. Everything starts with the word, and they know it.

Unfortunately, this puts writers in the crosshairs of every con man, user, abuser, self-described agent, producer, and publisher on the planet. Anyone can hang out a shingle, print business cards, or create websites proclaiming their very important title to the world without having a single credit to back it up. Most of these are untalented amateurs who know that the only way to become what they *say* they are is to sink their teeth into someone who *does* have talent and exploit the hell out of them. You are all that stands between them and fortune, so they will do whatever is necessary to get you on board. They will dangle opportunities and lists of impressive connections to Important People, taking advantage of your naiveté, enthusiasm, and inexperience to get you to work without pay or with the understanding that payment is "deferred," just for a little while, of course. They will expect you to put in long hours giving them what they need, but if you ask for even the slightest bit of compensation, they will turn sullen and resentful, or in the case of the more slick operatives, fast-talk their way out of it. *Just keep going, I have a guy at Universal who's hot to read this, it's a sure sale. Once we get them a little pregnant and they want it, we can ask for anything, the sky's the limit.*

Of course you never get to *meet* these studio executives, because the person you're dealing with doesn't have those connections, which is why these "opportunities" invariably end up going nowhere. In the end, it's the writer who pays the price in sweat equity, wasting days, weeks, and months on projects that turn to vapor, followed by calls and texts sent to procure payment or clarity that are no longer returned.

Swimming in the ocean is fun and exciting and illuminates our understanding of the world and ourselves; but if we are wise, some part of our brain is always conscious of the fact that when we enter the sea, we are entering the food chain. Similarly, the moment you announce to the world that you're a writer open for business, you are entering the food chain, and the sharks will begin circling almost immediately.

The moment anyone tries to entice you into writing something for free or for little compensation by saying *It's a sure thing!* your first and immediate response should be to hit them in the face with a snow shovel, really hard, a lot.

I've briefly alluded to the following incident a few times over the years, but to build out the story in more detail: As the summer break before my last year in college began, I decided to begin work on a screenplay, some spec TV scripts, or maybe even get most of a novel down on paper. That summer was to be my gift to myself as a writer, and after three years of starving, scrimping, and saving whatever I could from selling small articles to local newspapers, I had *just* enough money to purchase that window of opportunity.

But before I could even begin, I was approached by a self-described "producer" who said he had seen some of my work and felt that I was the perfect fit for a feature film he wanted to develop. He had a rough idea for the movie—a heist story—but no more than that because he wasn't a writer. He told me that a host of important contacts were eager to see the project, and that he was absolutely certain he could get the film produced as soon as he had a script to work from because, again, *that's where everything starts.*

I hesitated, explaining that my plan was to use that summer to write the personal stories that could take my career to the next level, but he was quite insistent, and after some backing-and-forthing he finally put a contract in front of me. *I guess he's serious about this,* I thought. Now, I had never seen a writing contract before and had no idea what any of it meant, but it *looked* like a real contract and I was blinded by the line specifying the WGA minimum sale figure of $23,000 (from memory), which was ten times my yearly income as a writer.

Just to be clear, he wasn't offering to buy the script up front out of his own finances, only specifying what I'd get paid once he sold the project and the studio paid *him.* When I said that felt awfully speculative, he added a clause stipulating that if for whatever reason the project didn't sell—*But don't worry too much about that, Joe, like I said, it's a slam dunk*—he would pay me a $1,000 kill fee.

That seemed fair, so I signed the contract and spent the entire summer that I'd set aside for my own writing working on his screenplay. I'd turn in the latest iteration, he'd give me notes, and off I'd go to implement them. Draft after draft, week after week. Whenever I inquired about his contacts, he offered only vague generalities about executives who were "really excited" and kept asking when they'd be able to read the script.

I finished the last draft of the script just days before the next term was to begin. By now I'd gone through the limited funds I'd set aside for that summer and had to borrow money from friends to make rent, and loans from the state of California to cover tuition. But that didn't matter because the script was done, and since everyone wanted to see it and buy it and make the movie, I'd soon be rolling around in $23,000!

Weeks passed. Then months. Nothing. Messages left on his answering machine went unanswered. At the one-year mark, a time when I was facing extreme financial hardship, I asked for the kill fee. The project hadn't been sold, and the film hadn't been made, so I was owed the one grand, right?

Doesn't work that way, Joe, he said. *The terms of the kill fee state that it only gets paid when all good-faith efforts to sell the project have stopped. I'm still making those good-faith efforts.*[1]

The loss of that money at a time when I was in desperate need was a terrible blow, but what hurt even more was losing the precious time I'd set aside to write something for myself, scripts or stories that could have helped move my career along; it would be years before such an opportunity came again, and much crucial momentum was lost. The only resources a writer has to work with are time, energy, and visceral material, and the loss of all three that summer was devastating to me.

Another tale from the trenches:

Not long after arriving in Los Angeles, I began submitting samples of my work to agents in the hope of securing representation. One agent got back to me—I'll call her Cyndi but that's not her name—and during our meeting at a coffee shop in Beverly Hills she said she liked my samples and offered to send them around town to drum up work. She said that the more samples I gave her, the better my odds of breaking through, so I promised she'd get lots of material. She then gave me her card, a peck on the cheek, and her best wishes for what she believed would be a long and profitable partnership. In retrospect, I should have had the common sense to check out the address on her card more closely. Instead, I went happily on my way, sure that riches and fame were just around the corner.

Desperate to get something going, I spent almost *two years* writing spec scripts and sending them off in hopes of securing the promised meetings with story editors and studio development execs. Nothing happened. Follow-up calls to Cyndi's office always went to her phone service, after which she would call back to insist that it wasn't her fault that no meetings had occurred.

---

1 It is now forty years since that phone conversation, and I *still* haven't been paid, because the individual in question insists he is still making "good-faith efforts."

"All I can do is send the scripts out," she said. "If they're not good enough to get you meetings, then you need to write better."

It made sense, especially since I've always been very self-critical, so I kept going.

As more time passed without meetings, and the return calls came less frequently, I decided to pop by her office in Beverly Hills for the first time so we could discuss the matter in person. But when I reached the address, I couldn't find her office—there were just high-priced stores and a couple of small eateries. Then I noticed that the address on her card matched a mailbox and phone answering service. The Beverly Hills office to which I'd been sending spec scripts for nearly two years *didn't exist*.

Trying not to panic, I called Cyndi and again got the answering service. Without alluding to what I'd discovered, I said I was going to be in West Hollywood the next day and invited her to lunch, my treat. She left word later that afternoon to confirm that she'd be there.

She arrived first, and when she saw my expression as I entered, her smile faded quickly. After telling her what I had discovered in Beverly Hills, she reluctantly confessed that, no, she didn't have an office, that she'd never *had* an office; she was still trying to start her career as an agent. She hadn't told me any of this because in order for her to become successful she had to have clients, and nobody would sign with her knowing she was just starting out.

There had been no meetings with story editors or studio executives because she lacked the connections to get my material in front of anyone who could actually buy them. Rather than admit this, she kept coming back to ask for more and better material, putting the blame on me.

I was furious.

"I don't see what you're being so self-righteous about," she said. "I mean, *you're* new, too—you're looking for *your* first break—so what's the difference? We're both in the same boat."

That actually made sense for about ten seconds before I exploded. The only reason agents exist is to provide access to buyers. Cyndi didn't have access to the corridors of power. She didn't even have access to the *parking lots* of power. So I broke off the arrangement, told her to send back my material, and stormed out. Unfortunately, most of the TV shows for which I'd written spec scripts were off the air not long afterward, rendering them useless as samples and forcing me to start all over again.

Such experiences are not unique to me or to the period in which they took place.

They continue to happen right now, today, this very minute.

Last year, another self-described producer asked the daughter of a friend of mine to help him create a new streaming video series, based on his idea (see prior screed), which he would sell to YouTube or the now defunct online short-form streamer Quibi. He felt that in order to do this right and guarantee a sale (there's always a guarantee, isn't there?) she would need to write the entire first season up front: fifteen episodes at ten minutes each. One hundred and fifty minutes equals 180 pages, but with no money up front. *Don't worry, as soon as I can get this to my people, we're golden.*

Over the course of six months, she wrote five drafts, most of them page-one rewrites, in order to meet his notes and incorporate his ideas. Five drafts times 180 pages equals 900 pages worth of writing not counting outlines and a series bible that he decided would help push them over the edge into a sale. She worked on this to the exclusion of everything else, even quitting one of her part-time jobs to invest more time into the writing process, a decision that forced her to fast twice a week to save money on food.

The project went nowhere. The vaunted contacts did not exist, the series was never sold, she never earned a penny, and worst of all there's nothing she can do with the material she wrote. Even though there was no contract—at this stage there rarely is—the scripts incorporated his ideas, so as far as he's concerned he owns it, and threatened to sue her if she tries to take it anywhere else. An attorney she consulted said he owns *half* of it, but that's enough to tie up the property in court indefinitely. The result: six months wasted and nine hundred dead pages. Nine hundred pages is two novels, seven-and-a-half screenplays, seventeen hour-long TV scripts, or about forty-five short stories. Gone. Like that. Gone.

And it happens every day.

Hey, I'm putting together a new website for creators, there's gonna be big money down the road but right now I'm desperate for content so if you could just write me a few articles for free I can make it up to you later when this hits big . . .

My brother works for a big publishing company and he's looking for an international thriller to turn into a best seller. I have the story but I need someone to write the book with me and I can bring it to him and I know he'll buy it and . . .

I'm producing a low-budget film but the script doesn't work, so if you rewrite it for me I can pay you a full script fee once I sell it to the film festival circuit . . .

I want to use Kickstarter to finance a series of short films and there's no money at the start for anyone, but if it takes off the way I expect, we'll be rolling in it. We just need to get the scripts out there where the investors can see them. Yeah, you're taking a chance, but I'm taking a chance, too, so . . .

You hear that last one a lot in this business. They say, *Hey, I'm taking a chance on this so why shouldn't you?* despite the fact that it's a producer's *job* to take chances. It's a writer's job to get paid for work done. It's like pulling into a gas station and saying, *Hey, listen, I'm up for a big job in Austin that'll pay me tons of money but I need to get there for the interview so if you could just give me a tank of gas I'll pay you when I get the job.*

Writers are naïve and enthusiastic because we dream big, confident that at any moment our work is going to trigger some vast life-changing event, so when someone comes at us with wild promises of success and money, we desperately want to believe them. That's why it's essential to protect yourself by taking a few simple commonsense steps. If these basic safeguards annoy the other party, if they get defensive or run away, that means they were going to take advantage of you and changed their mind only when they realized that you knew what you were doing. Consider it shark repellent for dry-land predators.

The most important thing is to do your due diligence. Force them to be *specific*, then follow up on that information. If they say they have a certain job description or a studio deal, look it up online. In these days of 24/7 social media and entertainment press, every deal gets announced someplace where you can find it.

If they say they have an important connection, get a name. If they get cranky, if they say, *Look, either you trust me or you don't; if not, I'll just find someone else,* this confirms that they were going to take advantage of you. If you can be switched out that easily for another writer, then you're not as uniquely qualified as they insisted, and they're relying more on your naiveté than your skills. They want people who can be easily scammed, and if that's not you they'll move on to an easier target of opportunity.

Any professional agent, producer, publisher, or manager will happily provide bona fides to back up their assertions because they know that there are hundreds of fakes out there making them look bad by association. If anything, they'll respect that you're proceeding in a businesslike fashion. Everybody checks out everybody else. If you're a producer or show-runner and you're considering hiring a particular crew member or actor, you *always* call the last three folks he or she worked for to get the lowdown. I've made that call, I've received that call, and on occasion I've been the subject of that call. Agents call agents, publishers call publishers, and producers call producers to find out if you're the real deal. And they fully expect you to do the same.

On the other hand, if the other party *does* trust you with the name of an associate, never call that person to say, *Hey, do you know so-and-so?* because being that blatant makes you both look bad. Instead, call under the guise of introducing yourself rather than verifying that the other person is who they say they are. *Hey, I ran into so-and-so over drinks at Trader Vic's last night, and it looks like we're going to be working together on a project he wants to bring to you, so he suggested I call to introduce myself. Yeah, I agree, he's a great, stand-up guy. We're hoping to have something to show you next month. Anyway, I don't want to hold you up; I just wanted to say hello and introduce myself. Have a great rest-of-your-day.*

The person on the receiving end of that call knows full well you weren't *really* calling to introduce yourself, and that's okay. That's how the game is played. What matters is that they know you're doing your homework, you know that the person you're working with is the real deal, and everybody's happy.

The same rule applies to contracts for writing assignments, options on material, or anything else that gets papered between the two of you. If you're not a lawyer, tell them that you'd like to run the contract past an attorney for an informed opinion. (Information on showbiz contracts is also available via the Writers Guild's website, www.wga.org.) If they try to discourage you, if they pressure you to sign *rightdamnitnow* or the offer goes away, if they play the *do you trust me or not* card . . . walk away.

Finally, as with any relationship, you should be proactive in making sure that all is as it should be. Visit them at their place of business and take them out to lunch. Learn what you can about them and strengthen the ties between you. That's not easy for some writers, because, let's face it, most of us are hermits, but it's absolutely necessary.

Bottom line: never take anyone's word for anything unless you've worked with them before or have checked them out thoroughly. Develop a healthy sense of skepticism. Don't get bitter, jaded, or distrustful, just approach every new situation with an attitude of professionalism and cautious optimism. When in doubt, follow your gut and put a proper value on your time, your talent, and your energy, because if you don't, no one else will.

Don't waste your golden summers chasing someone else's dream.

Because we don't get many of those.

HEARING VOICES

During an interview with the *Atlantic*, Stephen King said, "I can remember teaching *Dracula* to [high school] sophomores and practically screaming, 'Look at all the different voices in this book! Stoker's a ventriloquist! I love that!'"

In any work of fiction, the characters must sound and feel so distinct from one another, so unique, that you could cross out the names and still be able to tell who's talking. This is particularly true in *Dracula*, singled out by King because much of the novel is written in epistolary form: letters, journals, telegrams, and diary entries rather than a conventional narrative. Each entry is a different voice, a different style, a different way of thinking. But creating strong, individualized voices can be a struggle for new writers, whose characters often tend to sound the same. More specifically, they often end up sounding a great deal like the writer because at this stage most of us have only our own voice to work with.

Failing to create distinct characters renders them uninteresting and flattens the narrative. It's like being in a room with someone who keeps talking in a monotone, never raising his voice or changing inflection, just droning on endlessly; it's natural to lose interest. This applies equally to fiction: If everyone sounds the same, the narrative becomes monotonous and the reader stops paying attention to the details of the story, or worse still, gets bored and gives up.

While pursuing my Bachelor's Degree in sociology, I took a statistics-heavy course that was taught at the ungodly hour of eight a.m. by a gray little man in a gray suit with a gray little voice that never went up or down, just one long, flat, run-on sentence that would put many of his students to sleep, myself included. One morning, as the professor droned on in that sadistic monotone, I fell asleep *so hard* that I literally flipped the desk.[1] One minute I'm trying to keep my eyes open, the next I'm on the floor, under my desk.

"Are you all right?" the instructor asked as I crawled out from under the debris. "What happened?"

I couldn't say *your voice put me to sleep*, so my only defense was, "I, um . . . I tripped."

Many new writers will base their characters on friends, family, and others whose voices and personalities are sufficiently familiar to them to be able to mimic on the page. There are, however, three downsides to this.

First, creating original characters is fundamental to being a writer. It's fine to draw on friends and family in the beginning, when you don't know any other way, but if you allow this to become a habit you won't learn the necessary lessons about developing characters of your own. It's also a fair bet that most of the people we know tend to share our social, ethnic, and regional history, and that homogeneity can make the characters based on them feel too similar to one another. (That being said, sometimes you want all the characters in your story to share the same cultural wellspring or be members of the same family or social group. This might seem to simplify the process, but in fact it vastly complicates the writing because making such culturally intertwined characters sound unique from one other is substantially more difficult. Which is why the writing behind Tennessee Williams' *Cat on a Hot Tin Roof* is so exemplary: the characters grew up within a few miles of each other, but every voice is utterly and absolutely unique.)

Second, if you base your characters on people you know, and some of those characters are portrayed in a negative or libelous fashion, the folks who inspired those characters might get upset if they recognize themselves in the telling. You could get slugged, sued, or at minimum lose a friend.

---

1 Apparently maintaining a stable desk environment has been a recurring problem for me since high school.

Third, as much as knowing the real people behind your characters can serve as a safety line, it can also restrict you creatively. If you put that character into a situation where they have to do something that runs contrary to what that person would do in real life, a part of your brain starts to pump the brakes. You can probably force the writing process enough to get what you need for that scene, but the telling of it will ring false to the reader because it rings false to you.

Creating characters based primarily on those we know in real life is like using training wheels on a bike; they will help you learn balance, but you'll never get where you're going until you're willing to take them off and ride out under your own power. But if you're still not there yet, there's a technique (some might say it's a bit of a cheat but it works so I'm going to leave it here anyway) that can help: substitute well-known actors from TV and film for your characters.

We all know that Jimmy Stewart sounds very different from Tom Cruise who sounds very different from Steve Carell who sounds different from Will Smith. We know them so well that we can intuit not just what they might say in a given situation, but how they would say it, so you might as well use that knowledge to your benefit. Rather than writing the names of your characters, use the names of the actors whose personalities seem closest to them. As you go forward in the writing, this mental image will shade the dialogue and they will almost immediately begin to sound distinct from one another. Then, when you're finished, simply substitute the names of your characters for the names of the actors. It sounds dopey, but it can work as a stopgap measure during the early stages of your work. Remember, though, that the goal is to create your own characters end to end, and any cheat relied upon for too long will suck all the joy and innovation out of the writing process.

Choosing the right names for your characters can also help make their voices distinct. I can't count the number of scripts and stories I've read in which the names of the characters were little more than interchangeable placeholders. Bob, Jim, Sara, Tom . . . bland, boring names that blur into each other and tell the reader nothing about them. If you see these characters as being generic, that's how you will write them, and how the readers will perceive them. We tend to have certain notions about what a Karl looks like, or an Elijah; a Stella or a Zola; a Stanley or a Burt or a Nico.[2] A character who insists that her family members call her Elizabeth instead of Liz, resisting the least bit of informality even among those closest to her, tells you something about her personality that informs the writing. The names you choose should be evocative, interesting, and as much as possible, reflective of ethnically diverse backgrounds. We are a global, multicultural planet, and ensuring that your characters look and sound like the rest of the world will broaden the work.

To pursue that line of thought a bit further, another aid to creating distinct dialogue and characters is to set them against a geographic background that contrasts or complements the story you're trying to tell. The first season of HBO's *True Detective* series was heavily influenced by the stories of H. P. Lovecraft, and since Lovecraft set most of his fiction in New England, the simplest choice would have been to do the same, as many filmmakers have done over the years. Instead, the writers and producers set their story in the wilds of Louisiana, a location that gave the series a fresh feel and invested the characters with the rich history, language, accents, and vocabulary of the region.

Let's say you're writing a domestic drama about a soon-to-be-divorced husband who is having affairs around town and ends up being murdered for his transgressions. That story plays one way in the penthouse towers of Manhattan, and another way entirely in a tiny house along the Mississippi Delta or upstate Wisconsin. Think through your options, choose wisely, then load up on the texture of the locations through research. Writers are sponges; we pick up the flavor of whatever we're dumped into, so if you're writing a story based in Arkansas, read books and watch movies set in that location because the rhythms, word choices, and cadences will stay with you during the writing process.

When conveying dialect and accents, avoid trying to typographisize [I just made that word up and I regret nothing] their speech patterns. Don't

---

2 And for god's sake, if you're going to come up with an alien name for an off-world species, make it something that a reader or an actor can say without suffering an aneurysm. Nf'trxhdp may look nicely alien on the page, but spoken aloud or subvocalized repeatedly over potentially hundreds of pages almost certainly constitutes a violation of the Geneva War Crimes Convention, and if not, I make a motion.

write, "An' ah said to him, ah said General Sinclair, you dun' know the furst thing 'bout how t'fight a battle." That may seem obvious but you'd be surprised how many new writers do it. Bring out your character's voice with word choice, grammar, and syntax, not typosillinesses [no regrets about that one either]. Let their underlying attitudes, tone of voice, and sentence structure be your guide, flipping to specific terms, typography, or slang only when absolutely needed.

Finally, and maybe most importantly, as you begin to create the voices of your characters it's vital to remember that *you are not alone in that process*. You have a collaborator beside you the whole time who will eagerly leap into the fray to help define the voices in your story. I'm referring, of course, to the readers, because the moment you draw a picture in their minds, they will instinctively fill in the gap when it comes to accent, phraseology, diction, and voice.

Take for example the following line of dialogue: "I realize that this may be a bit of an inconvenience." On its own, it's anonymous, flat, and impersonal.

Now suppose the line is being spoken (and clearly I'm exaggerating for effect but bear with me) by Beauregard Hampton, an eighteenth-century southern gentleman. Got him in your head? Okay, now go back and read the sentence again as if he's saying it.

You heard it differently, didn't you?

Now switch it up and pretend the line is being spoken today by Devon Taylor, a member of the British intelligence service MI6. Go back and reread the sentence.

Changed again, yes?

Put the words in the mouth of a mafia don looking down at a guy tied up in the trunk of his car.

Now Mother Superior talking to a novitiate nun.

Now an interrogator in the former Soviet Union.

Every time you reread that sentence, knowing who was saying it produced a different voice in your head *even though the structure never changed*. Your brain automatically added the necessary inflections. Yes, some of these are extreme examples chosen to make the point, but the process is the same even with subtler or more finely tuned characters.

FINISH THE DAMNED THING

W hen lecturing at the same venues over several years, I often notice recurring faces, themes, and questions. *How do you get an agent? Where do you start a story? Which way is the bathroom? Do you work here? Why are you staring at me like that?* And the ever-popular *What's the most important piece of advice you would give to a new writer?*

The answer to that last one is always the same: "Finish it. Whatever you've started, whatever you're working on right now, finish the damned thing."

(Apparently I am sometimes more vociferous on this point than I realized. In a tweet posted September 19, 2018, a writer named Nicole Dubuc wrote, "At Comic Con in the early 2000s, I went to a Straczynski writing panel. His advice was 'finish it.' I must've audibly whimpered ['it' was a screenplay, stuck in act one], because he pointed at me, looked into my soul and said: 'You. FINISH IT.' Best advice ever." She then went on to write—and FINISH—scores of television scripts for network and syndicated series.)

The four essential rules of writing as expressed by Robert Heinlein are: (1) You must write, (2) you must finish what you write, (3) you must put it on the market, and (4) you must keep it on the market until sold.

Otherwise you end up like *this* guy:

Over the years, I've frequently been invited to speak as Guest of Honor at the Los Angeles Science Fiction Convention (Loscon). During these appearances, I noticed the same guy always sitting in the same seat in the first row, panel after panel, for *ten years*. He'd take advantage of his position at the front of the room to pepper me with writing questions. Some were infuriatingly vague, and others were specific to his own work, which obviously I had not seen and could not assess. Nevertheless, I tried to answer as best I could.

On more than one occasion I pulled him aside to ask that he be more courteous in letting others ask the occasional question rather than monopolizing the conversation for his own benefit, that there was a difference between *proximity* and *permission*. He always said he would endeavor to do so but rarely followed through. The last time I reprimanded him, my curiosity got the better of me and as he started to turn away I asked if my answers over the years had done him any good.

"I'm not sure," he said. "I'm still working on it."

It? *It?* He couldn't possibly mean what I thought he meant, could he?

He did. He had been working on the same novel for over a decade.

I pressed the point further, asking how much of the book had been completed.

He threw a bunch of words into the air in the hope that one of them would suffice, but by the time they settled back onto the ground it was clear he hadn't written a word.

Fighting to keep my blood pressure from stampeding toward a hypertensive crisis, I asked why the *hell* he had spent ten years asking questions that were of no use to anyone else, or that I had to put through a mental blender to turn into something that made sense, if he wasn't going to use any of that advice by actually *writing* something. In response he became defensive and agitated. How dare I question him?

"Here's the deal," I said in a voice like a tectonic rumble from the very bottom of the Mariana Trench. "You don't get to ask me any more questions."

"You can't stop me—"

"If you raise your hand, I'll ignore it. If you start to speak uninvited, I'll cut you off. Bad enough you're wasting my time. What's *truly* unforgivable is that you've wasted the time of everyone else in that room who has only a brief window in which to ask a question that could make a huge difference to their work and their future. I don't want to see you in the front row, or the back row, or any of the rows in between until you can walk in with a finished manuscript to prove to me that you're serious. If you can do that, great; otherwise, get outta my face."

He never came back.

Poseurs and pretenders get under my skin because they make it that much harder for anyone else who says *I'm a writer* to be taken seriously. And the biggest giveaway that you're dealing with a poseur rests at the heart of this chapter: finishing things. They talk a good game but at the end of the day, the page remains blank.

Fakes aside, let's turn our attention to some of the factors that lead many beginning writers to fall short of the finish line.

STAR SYNDROME

You don't need me (or this book) (or your friends) (or the people who *pretend* to be your friends just so they can pinch your weed) to tell you that we are living in Instagram America, whose borders are defined by selfies, Snapchats, Pinterest pages, hashtags, food photos, instant Twitter-born celebrity, and the desperate need to feel *important*. It helps if one has talent, but that's a difficult road because talent has to be proven. If someone says they're an actor, and you ask, *Have you actually done any acting?* and the person replies *No*, that's a pretty clear indication that the person is either lying or Nicolas Cage.

If someone says they're a doctor, they will be asked to produce their degree. A singer? Belt one out. Dancer? Dance. Painter or sculptor? Let's see some gallery photos.

But if someone else says, *I'm a writer*, and you ask, *Have you finished anything?* it's somehow socially acceptable for the person to say *No* and to even be offended by the question. Writing is one of the few professions where you don't have to *prove* you can do it to *say* that you do it. *I'm still working on my writing . . . I have tons of talent, I just want to be sure the work is up to my standards . . . I'm typing at a Starbucks so obviously I'm a movie writer and any moment now my words will be recognized for pure gold.*

Such individuals lay claim to talents they don't possess because it's hard to contest their assertions without seeming rude. This gives them the benefit of some small measure of fame within their circle of friends and family . . . and if it's possible to get the regard given to a writer without having to do the work required to actually *finish* something, then really, why bother?

JUDGE NOT

At the other end of the spectrum are those who genuinely want to be writers and are willing to put in the effort necessary to learn their craft, but still find themselves unable to finish things. They'll start one project only to toss it aside to work on something else, which *also* goes unfinished. They'll say that the dialogue isn't working, the characters need to be further refined, they're tightening the plot, or they just don't have the time to finish it right now. And it's entirely possible that some or all of those may even be true, but they can't all be true *consistently*; the math alone dictates that sooner or later the stars have to align, lighting the way to completion at least *once* in a while, unless there's something *else* going on beneath the surface, a problem that has little to do with story construction and everything to do with fear.

Writing, like any other form of art, exposes us to the world in profoundly personal ways. Whatever doubts we may have about our abilities are heightened at the prospect of having our work seen by others. As long as the work is in progress, no one can say, *This is terrible*. It's only when we finish and show it to someone that it can be judged, and our talent along with it. As with Schrödinger's Cat, as long as the story remains unfinished in the box, neither it nor you as an artist can be judged. It's only when you pull the story out of the box and allow it to be read that those two quantum probabilities fold into one quantum reality, and you're either a skilled writer with a career, or you suck.

If your inability to finish the work arises from a fear of being judged, one solution is to avoid presenting it to someone as a *fait accompli*. If you say, *This is the story—it's done and it's not going to be changed; so what do you think?* you're telling the reader that you're not receptive to suggestions or criticisms. Since they can't give you a proper critique, their only remaining option is an up-or-down, success-or-fail referendum on your talent, which is exactly what you're trying to avoid at this point.

A better approach, even if you honestly think that the story's finished, is to tell the reader that you're between first and second revisions, and that you'd love to hear any suggestions that can improve the next iteration. This gives you, the reader, and your talent more wiggle room than saying, *This is the final, truest representation of my talent and my true self—have I got it or not?*

Another solution is to finish the work *without* immediately showing it to anyone. Just type THE END, internalize whatever lessons that particular work had to teach you, and move on to the next story. By the time you finish several more projects, you will be able to go back to the first one with fresh eyes and improve it through revision. Waiting a while also makes it easier to give that first work to someone for their opinion because by now you've moved on to the next story. Your identity as an artist isn't as thoroughly tied into that one work because there are now several others lined up behind it.

PERFORMANCE ANXIETY

Sometimes our desire to finish the story bumps up against our desire for perfection. We say it's not ready, it needs more work, it needs to be *perfect*, and the editing process turns into a never-ending loop driven by the hope that *this* time we'll get it right. But *perfect* is the enemy of *good*, because perfection is unattainable. The goal should be to bring the work along until it is acceptable, then good, and then the best you can make it at this stage of your ability, then leave it alone and move on to the next thing. Because however much effort you put into it, the work will never even be *acceptable* if you don't finish it. As da Vinci (allegedly) said, "Art is never finished, only abandoned."

In confronting one's fear of imperfection, remember the Secret of the Persian Rug. It's said that the very finest rug makers always include one small flaw in the finished work, because otherwise the work would be perfect, and that would offend God, because only God can create perfection. Viewed in that light, the imperfections in your work not only make you unique, they help you avoid offending God, which means you may have saved the world from a premature apocalypse, and how many people can say that?

Whatever your fears or motivations, when you as a beginning writer give your work to someone for their opinion, keep in mind that neither you nor your talent are being judged in the long term. A story or a script is merely a photograph of where you are as an artist at a particular moment; it is not prophecy. Art is incremental, growing and changing as we do. A bad review is not revealed truth, and often has little bearing on the quality of the work produced tomorrow or the day after. If your art isn't where you need it to be, just keep writing. With time, you *will* improve. It's inevitable. I defy *anyone* to write ten short stories and not have story #10 be at least incrementally better than #1.

But it all starts with the end.

So finish the damned thing.

HILLS, VALLEYS, AND THE REFRACTORY PERIOD

Make it dark, make it grim, make it tough, but then, for the love of god, tell a joke.
Joss Whedon

t's a natural impulse.

I'm writing a horror movie, so it should be scary end to end.

I'm writing a comedy so it should be nonstop funny from start to finish.

It's also incorrect.

Any time you elicit a reaction from your reader or audience—terror, laughter, and all points in-between—it's a form of release, of catharsis. It is the top of the mountain. But you can't truly appreciate the view if all you see are other mountaintops. To get the full impact you need to look up at it from the ground once in a while. You work your way up, inch by inch, leading up to the moment when you crest the top with a serious or funny Big Moment of catharsis that releases the tension built up along the way. After that, you have to throttle back a little before you can begin rebuilding the tension. It's a kind of refractory period. . . you need a moment to catch your breath, have some Gatorade, talk about life, play the "How many bridges can you name?" game (the correct answer is four), *then* you can move on to the next Big Moment.

Writing is about peaks and valleys, about the moments *between* the moments. If you've just written a scary scene, follow it with a deeply personal scene that gives the prior scene greater meaning, lets the audience recover, and prompts them to begin worrying that the danger seen earlier might come after the characters we now care about even more than before.[1] A humorous moment sandwiched between two scary scenes makes the comedy funnier and the coming danger more impactful.

There *has* to be contrast.

If everything is funny, nothing is funny.

If everything is sad, nothing is sad.

If everything is scary, nothing is scary.

Going for the same reaction repeatedly flattens the story rather than making it more intense; the characters and situations get lost in the sense of overwhelming sameness. The best way to keep your audience engaged is to make sure that they don't know what's coming next. Readers and audiences love to be surprised, provided that the surprise makes sense within the parameters of your story and the characters you've established. The reason the Korean film *Parasite* generated so much press and walked away with the Academy Award for Best Picture was that you had no idea where it was going or what would happen next, creating tons of peaks and valleys as new information and relationships were revealed.

One of the best ways to keep your work from devolving into repetitive, one-note storytelling is to continually make unexpected but logical choices.

To explain via a different metric: Casting is one of the chief responsibilities of a television show-runner. This means sitting in a small, stuffy room with other executives and the casting director as five to ten actors competing for the same role enter, one at a time, to perform the same scene. The process can be agonizing because in preparing for their auditions, most of the actors make the obvious choices. The character's a bad guy, so the actor does the audition with a villainous snarl. Another character

---

1 There's a saying among some French film critics that the difference between a grade A film and a grade B film is that, in a B film, sex is followed by death as punishment, and in an A film, death is followed by sex as affirmation. Following this line of thought to its inevitable conclusion, the combination of sex and death together is followed mainly by the French.

is the comic relief, so the actor plays the humor and chews every piece of scenery in sight. So you're hearing the same words, spoken in very similar ways, courtesy of the obvious choices, over and over and over for hours.

But then something miraculous happens, and an actor brings you the unexpected choices. The nominal bad guy is played with a sly sense of humor or paternal affection; the "comic relief" is played with vulnerability or sadness or even a touch of unanticipated rage at always having to *be* the funny guy . . . and suddenly the whole room lights up and everyone's paying attention. Nine times out of ten, *that's* the actor who gets the job.

The more your work can exhibit surprising, unexpected choices that still manage to make sense within the context of your story, the greater the odds that it will grab the attention of an editor, publisher, or producer.

Another way in which stories can become one-note is by ending on their premise, setting up situations worthy of exploration but failing to develop them to their maximum potential. It's a hard concept to explain, but once you get it, you Get It for life. So let me illustrate by way of the most obvious example of this I've ever seen, even though doing so means going back in time a little.

In the mid-1980s, NBC ran an anthology series entitled *Amazing Stories* produced by Universal Studios and based on the magazine of the same name. (A new iteration of the series is currently airing in 2020 as I write this, so the topic is more timely than it might at first appear.) During that same period, I was working on *The Twilight Zone* series, and in the spirit of full disclosure I must admit that there was a bit of a rivalry between the shows. Where *TZ* emphasized strong writers, *Amazing Stories* defaulted to well-known directors who provided much of the show's creative vision. But directors are not necessarily writers, and it requires more than a good eye to develop stories with a compelling beginning, middle, and end. Consequently, many of the episodes were paper-thin at best. When a journalist asked what I thought of the series, I replied, in a moment of puckishness, "My problem with *Amazing Stories* is that it's neither."

After taking a moment to process the syntax, he got the joke, laughed, and printed the article, resulting in several highly annoyed phone calls from Universal.

The problem, for me, was that many of the episodes ended on their premise. In "Gather Ye Acorns" a troll convinces the main character that he shouldn't give up his comic book collection because someday it will save him. Thirty years and twenty-seven minutes of broadcast time later, he gets in a jam and sells his comics for a ton of money because, by golly, it turns out that they massively accrued in value during the interim. The end is what the beginning was predicated upon, and what was stated in the beginning is exactly what happens at the end.

But the most egregious example was "Ghost Train," which featured an old man named Opa Globe who, at the top of the episode, states his belief that, well, a *ghost train* called the Highball Express is going to come to take him to the other side. His friends and family spend the next twenty-two minutes trying to convince him that there's no such thing as a Ghost Train, and no way is anything like that coming to take him to the other side. No, no, he insists, the Ghost Train is real, and it's going to come and take him to the other side.

Sure enough, at the twenty-seven-minute mark, the Ghost Train comes for him and takes him to the other side.

That's the story.

No, seriously, that's the story.

Premise: *The Ghost Train is coming for me.*

End: *Welp, it's here.*

It ends on its premise.

The presence of a beginning, middle, and end does not mean that the story actually develops, or that it has done more with its premise than simply state its existence. It's a common problem for new writers, who will be hit by what they think is an amazing idea, a revelation, a striking scene or an image. They put it down on paper complete with words and dialogue and punctuation but without making interesting choices about how to develop it further, which means *it's not a story*. It's a *premise* for a story that's been *mistaken* for a story.

The writer's task is to take readers someplace *new* where we can explore the emotional highs and lows of your story right there alongside your characters, experiencing the consequences of your art like an almost-out-of-control roller coaster. Don't write in a monotone, end on your premise, or only make the obvious choices.

Make the unexpected choices. Surprise us.

QUESTIONS OF INTENT

Director Mike Nichols once said, "There are only three kinds of scenes: negotiations, seductions, and fights." I'm not sure that's correct—I've never embraced the kind of reductionist thinking that has to stipulate even the smallest disagreement as a fight in order to justify such distinctions—but I'm not sure he's entirely wrong either. Pulling back to a helicopter view of that statement, I think Mr. Nichols was pointing to the importance of *intent*.

At risk of telling you what you already know, every work of fiction, whether a prose novel or a screenplay, is made up of scenes. But beginning writers sometimes forget that those scenes must be more than tools designed to get you from Plot Point A to Plot Point B. Just as every note in a song or symphony matters, every scene in a work of fiction is important because *every scene is a story unto itself*, with a beginning, middle, and end, and needs to be written accordingly. As Michelangelo once wrote, "Trifles make perfection, and perfection is no trifle."

And it all comes down to intent.

In preparing to write a novel or screenplay, you are expected to work out the motivations of your characters, what they want, what they're afraid of, and what the story is ultimately about. But that rule applies as much to the micro scale as it does to the macro. Before committing a scene to pen and paper (or keyboard and program), you have to ask not just what purpose a given scene serves in the narrative, but what is the story of the scene itself?

Writing a story at length is like rolling a ball down a snow-covered mountain. The more details it picks up along the way, the bigger it grows and the greater the impact when it lands. But if it hits a patch of ground where there's no snow, nothing to hold on to, and nothing new that gets added, the whole thing starts to break apart. The result is the same if your reader hits a scene that doesn't add anything to their understanding of the story or the characters, a scene that's just sort of *there*. Yes, Character A must meet Character B in this scene in order for their relationship to develop later, but it has to be more than just an introduction or a conversation without consequence. *Hi, yeah, good to meet you. I hope you find your stay here comfortable. If you need anything, let me know. Well, gotta go. Have a great day.*

Every time you write a scene, you have to ask what Character A wants to find out or achieve, even if A doesn't know that when the scene begins. It's fine for A to go into the scene with a clear-cut agenda, which motivates the action, or to discover that intent during the scene, which allows the reader to participate in a shared moment of discovery, but either way, that intent has to be there. Conversely, you also have to work out what Character A does *not* want to reveal in the course of that conversation. Is A attracted to B but trying not to show it? Or is s/he repelled? Is A trying not to show secret joy at a *faux pas* committed by B? Does A suddenly realize that B is connected to a pivotal part of the overall story in unexpected ways, and must now be careful to avoid tipping their hand and risk being harmed?

Once you've answered those questions, you have to do the same for Characters B and C. What do *they* want to get out of this conversation, and what do they *not* want? It needn't be a world-shattering secret, but there has to be some underlying emotion or intent that will stick to the ever-growing snowball and make the scene more than an information dump. Plan out *how* your characters get into the scene, their *reason* for being there, what they get *out* of it, what they don't want the *other* party to get out of it, and where they come out the other side. This gives the scene purpose and dramatic tension. Lacking those elements, the scene should be cut.

The intentions of your characters need not be shouted as long as they're present inside your head during the writing process; they can be put forth quietly, implied, or communicated through subtext. In every dialogue exchange, there's what a character is *saying*, what they're *not* saying, and what they're *really* saying when they're allegedly talking about something else. Intent can be as much about what the characters refuse to discuss as what they do, as much about withholding information as gathering it, which goes back to what Nichols said about negotiations, seductions, and fights. Character A may enter the scene intent on making Character B acknowledge paternity, or to reveal that he or she is gay, but if Character B refuses to acknowledge any of that information, then the competing intentions clash into dramatic conflict.

One of the joys of a play by Harold Pinter comes from watching the characters spend a lot of time talking about everything except the matter at hand, but doing so in such a way that they're only and always ever talking about that one thing. Writing of the power of silence in his work, Pinter said that "in our silence, in what is unsaid, what takes place is a continual evasion, desperate rearguard attempts to keep ourselves to ourselves because communication is too alarming. To enter into someone else's life is too frightening. To disclose to others the poverty within us is too fearsome a possibility."

Writing characters who are incapable or unwilling to confront the truth between them adds significantly to the tension because after a while you're just waiting for one of them to explode.

While I was getting my degree in psychology at San Diego State University, we were told about a man who was tying his shoes one day when the shoelace snapped, and he went catatonic. Now, obviously, he didn't really snap over a broken shoelace; the event was triggered by what the shoelace *represented*, becoming a symbol for all the pain and loss and disappointments he had recently suffered, for which a broken shoelace was the one more thing he just couldn't handle. The shoelace was the metaphor, the subtext, for all that preceded it.

So, in addition to all the things that your characters can say that will reveal intent, there's also the matter of what they're thinking about but *not* expressing directly, the shoelace waiting to snap, emotional and psychological underpinnings to the dialogue that can allow the audience to derive different shades of meaning from what's actually being said.

Imagine a party scene where someone's wife finally meets the woman she believes is having an affair with her husband. She can't prove the affair and doesn't want to make a scene in front of a crowd, which mitigates against direct confrontation. But everything she says to her rival—about how she's dressed, is she seeing anyone, and isn't everyone just so happy to be here—has a double meaning for her, for her rival, and for the audience. And the other woman is doing the same in reverse. To anyone looking on without knowing the context, it seems like any other conversation, but the tension is palpable to the audience, who are in on the subtext, and are on the edge of their seats waiting for one of them to throw a punch or a drink.

As an exercise, write a scene where the wife is talking to her husband about the party the next day. She wants to see his reaction to what happened, and he wants to find out how much she knows or suspects, but neither one of them can come out and directly express what they're *really* talking about. Dig into the scene to see how long you can realistically extend it.

As an alternate exercise, write a scene that takes place after a horrendous argument between two lovers. Neither party wants to light that up again, but echoes and resentments of the fight linger behind every word and glance.

Or a scene where someone is trying to decide whether or not it's safe to confide to their parents that s/he is bisexual, and is framing the dinner conversation with carefully worded questions in order to get a sense of the terrain. The possibilities, like stories themselves, are endless.

As you write, remember that people occupy physical space, regardless of whether they exist onstage or only in the reader's mind. Space, physicality, and narrative direction can communicate as much intent and subtext as language.

Visualize a young couple standing in the kitchen, inches apart. *I love you*, he says. A simple, declarative sentence. Not much that we can do with it. Or is there?

He smiles and touches her hair as he says it. *I love you.* Sincere.

Now he's not smiling, and he's holding her arm a little too tightly. *I love you.* The subtext is that he's controlling. Fixated.

He's crying. *I love you.* She's leaving him.

Variation: *Of course I love you.* When he says it, the description tells us that his eyes have a wounded, sad look to them. She's jealous or fearful. He's trying to save the relationship.

He smiles as he says it. *Of course I love you*. He's being patronizing. Dismissive of her concerns.

He says it from across the room, his back turned to her. *Of course I love you*. Someone's heart is about to get broken.

The more physical details you can inject into a scene to give it dimensionality, energy, and subtext, the more the scene will shine with intent, further engaging the reader.

Someone once suggested that no Union or Confederate soldier ever saw the Civil War; they saw only their small part of it, the few feet of ground in front of them as they fought for their lives. That small window is where everything in your story takes place. *Stories* can be big, sprawling events, but *scenes* are all about the details, about the few feet in front of them, because that's where your characters live. A story is a fictional construct that strings events together to create meaning; characters exist within the scenes that make *up* that story more so than in the totality of the story because they can't see it. All they can do is live those moments, microsecond by microsecond, creating something bigger than they are with every word, deed, and gesture, line by line and breath by breath. That's why it's so important to plan out your scenes with as much precision as the overall arc of the story.

Trifles make perfection, and perfection is no trifle.

HOW TO BUILD A MONSTER
IN THREE EASY LESSONS

t goes without saying (so why I'm saying it is anyone's guess) that most writers identify with the heroes of their stories. Which is not to say that writers *can't* identify with their antagonists, only to suggest that if the character you relate to most in your story is the axe-wielding maniac who decimates an entire hospital and takes up two parking spots while doing it, a degree of self-reflection might be in order.

Audiences also tend to identify with the hero of the story, and want to see him or her triumph over adversity, bad luck, limited resources, and, ultimately, the bad guy.

Too often, however, the antagonist is *designed to be defeated*, nowhere near as smart, capable, or skilled as our hero. This is pernicious on many levels, leading to convenient storytelling, lack of credible conflict, and two-dimensional characters. If the audience knows that the bad guy is a clod and the hero is certain to win, they're just marking time until it happens. Yes, logically we know that, in the end, the protagonist is probably going to come out on top, and that good will triumph over evil; the fun is seeing how they pull it off given the magnitude of what they're up against.

The protagonist of Mary Shelley's *Frankenstein* was a scientist brilliant enough to storm the walls of Death and return with the secret of restoring life to inanimate flesh. With the odds so clearly stacked in his favor, the story could only work if the antagonist was equally smart and supremely strong. So in the novel (as opposed to the movies, which made his creation almost unintelligible), Frankenstein's creation is as literate as his creator and ridiculously difficult to kill.

(Quick sidebar: For five years I hosted a talk show on KPFK-FM Los Angeles called *Hour 25* where I was honored to be able to interview a wide range of writers, actors, directors, and producers. One of our guests was Curt Siodmak, a writer who had worked for Universal during its heyday, and had been deeply engaged in writing the original Frankenstein movie series, among others. He said that for himself and the other writers, one of the most enjoyable parts of working on Universal's slate of monster movies was, in his words, "rat-fucking the guy who came next." One writer would end his script by having the Monster disappear into a burning windmill, his way of saying to the others, "Write your way out of *that*!" The next writer would have to figure out how the Monster survived the inferno, then at the end of the script screw over the *next* writer by dropping the Monster into a frozen river, putting him in a tower as it explodes, burying him beneath a cave-in, and so on. Writers are funny critters.)

Superman is arguably the most powerful comic book character ever created, but there's no story tension if he can simply muscle himself out of any situation. This led to the creation of smart or massively powerful characters like Brainiac and Lex Luthor, who became some of his most enduring enemies. Similarly, Batman is famously "the world's greatest detective," so the writers at DC needed someone who was his equal, a character he could push against without the certitude of victory, so they created the Joker, who was nearly as brilliant but also insane, which made him almost impossible to predict, defeating Batman's logical mind.

Clarice Starling is the protagonist of *The Silence of the Lambs*, but it's the terrifying and brilliant mind of antagonist Hannibal Lecter that drives the story, pushing her to do things she would never have attempted on her own.

There are some who fear that making the antagonist too strong weakens the hero by comparison, but this could not be further from the truth. The stronger the bad guy, the more rewarding the hero's journey when he or she overcomes them. Heroes are defined by what they fight *for*, and who they are willing to fight *against* when no one else will take up the challenge. It's about what they stand for when standing is the hardest, and a strong antagonist can make that decision very hard indeed.

Colonel Kurtz in *Apocalypse Now*, Ahab in *Moby Dick*, Professor Moriarty in the Sherlock Holmes stories, Darth Vader in *Star Wars*, the Wicked Witch of the West in *The Wizard of Oz*, Roy Batty in *Blade Runner*, Lord Voldemort in the Harry Potter stories, Nurse Ratched in *One Flew over the Cuckoo's Nest*, Antonio Salieri in *Amadeus*, and King Richard in Shakespeare's *Richard III* have become cultural icons because of the care that the writers took in making them every bit as powerful and resourceful as our heroes.

The mathematics needed to achieve this are fairly straightforward. No matter how smart or strong your hero is, the other guy must be smarter and stronger. However far your hero is prepared to go, the enemy will go farther. If your hero lives mainly in his head, so that emotion is his blind spot, the antagonist is all emotion, impulse, and instinct. If your character is all about heart, the antagonist is cold and calculating. But those are just starting points. To be truly successful at creating worthy antagonists, we must go deeper.

It's altogether possible that an antagonist is consciously evil, fully aware that he is doing the wrong things for the wrong reasons, but it can be far more interesting if he has convinced himself that he's doing the wrong things for the *right* reasons, because that makes him infinitely more dangerous. Thanos in 2018's *Avengers: Infinity War* genuinely believed that he was trying to create a better future by depopulating whole worlds so that the surviving billions could rebuild with greater resources. Throughout the movie, he shows compassion, loss, and mercy, which makes him compelling and three-dimensional. Similarly, in *The Godfather*, Michael Corleone starts out determined to steer clear of the family's business in organized crime. But despite his best intentions, every step taken to protect his family, every choice made for what genuinely feels like the right reason, moves him further down that dark road until he becomes the very thing he hates.

The monster rarely sees a monster in the mirror. We are all the heroes of our own stories, and we all do what we do for the same reason: it seemed like a good idea at the time. So, as important as it is to figure out the motivations of the protagonist, an equal or even greater amount of time must be invested into figuring out who the antagonist is, why he or she is doing what they're doing, and what that goal means to them. Let them rationalize their actions so they feel they are on the right side of history (even though they may be very much on the other side), or that they're only doing these unfortunate things because it's necessary, and that they have no other choice.[1]

That word, *choice*, is central to the process of creating both your hero and your villain. Confronted by difficult or tempting circumstances, your characters must make a conscious decision to embrace the better or darker angels of their nature. They must be active, not passive, moving the story forward with their choices rather than letting the story push them around. This in turn gives you access to the Most Holy Trinity of story development: choice, consequence, and responsibility.

Choice. In storytelling, as in real life, we have the power to choose how we respond to a given situation. Our decision to choose the easy path or the hard path, and the reasons involved, can tell you a lot about the person making that choice. There is also much depth to be plumbed when someone rejects change or responsibility, insisting that they don't have a choice. Choice is *always* possible. The moment someone says *I have no choice*, they've *made* a choice, they just don't want to admit it to the other characters or to themselves. We can choose to do (1) the right things for the right reasons, (2) the right things for the wrong reasons, (3) the wrong things for the wrong reasons, or (4) the wrong things for the right reasons. Options 2 and 4 can be very useful in producing antagonists who are deeply conflicted about their identities and their choices.

Option 4, doing the wrong thing for the right reason, can also be used to make the hero of the story more interesting. In the aftermath of World War Two, a story emerged—supported by some historians, disputed by others—that in November 1941, British intelligence, armed with a captured German code machine referred to as Enigma, learned that the Luftwaffe was going to launch a devastating attack on the English city of Coventry. Over five hundred bombers would be used in the attack, with devastating implications for loss of life. The obvious response would have been to evacuate Coventry, but Churchill knew that showing prior knowledge of

---

1 Old saying of unknown parentage: "Rationalizations are more important than sex, because you can actually *go* a day without sex."

the attack would reveal that they had captured Enigma. This would make the Germans switch to a new coding system, a move that would almost certainly result in defeat for the Allies. So, according to the story, Churchill decided that for the greater good he would allow the bombing of Coventry to proceed. Was it the right thing for the wrong reason? The wrong thing for the right reason? Or a little of both?

Consequence. Once your characters make their choices, something good or bad must happen as a result or there's no reason to have that choice in the first place. While there's always room for the theater of paralysis as realized by such playwrights as Samuel Beckett, most stories require the negation of inertia, creating states of change that have profound effects on the characters. Protagonists can make choices that they hope will have positive consequences for themselves and others, leading to stories about personal growth or triumph. Antagonists can make choices they believe will have positive consequences for themselves at the cost of negative consequences for someone else, decisions that lend themselves to stories about conspiracies or dangers that force the hero to step out of their inertia in order to save others.[2] The latter is easier to structure and sell, which is why so many books and movies start with *the bad guy has a plan and we have to stop him* as a way to activate the hero rather than start with the hero saying *I am going to go out there and make the world a better place.* Since it's often the antagonist, rather than the hero, who is the story's prime mover, it's essential to ensure that the character's motivations are rock-solid.

Responsibility. Antagonists frequently try to shrug off the burden of responsibility for their actions to avoid feelings of guilt; protagonists often know nothing else. How each side processes responsibility reveals character in ways that reinforce their role in the story. The hero doesn't want people to get hurt, or if they do get hurt, accepts the emotional pain that results, becoming even more determined to bring down the bad guy. The bad guy

2 Academics sometimes point to *Rocky* as a story about personal growth and triumph, and while that's true for how it *ends*, it's not true for how it *begins*. Rocky exists in a state of inertia until acted upon by the story's antagonist, Apollo Creed. It's only after Rocky is activated as a hero—he wants a fight, okay, I'm gonna give him a fight and I'm gonna go the distance—that the growth process begins.

usually doesn't care if anyone gets hurt in the pursuit of his objectives, or if he does care, tries to blame others for his own actions. But there's something very interesting, less clichéd, when an antagonist makes his choices believing that they are correct, suffers through the consequences of those choices, and accepts responsibility for the resultant harm. Using the elements of choice, consequence, and responsibility in different combinations can be a huge help in creating three-dimensional antagonists.

Another way to create a well-rounded bad guy is to approach the problem from the other side, a method I call *Turning your hat around*, second-cousin to *Turning it upside down*, a technique discussed elsewhere.

Once you hit the end of your script or story, put it in a drawer and leave it there for a week. Don't take it out to revise it or bask in its majesty because that will just keep you in the mindset of the hero, and you need to be able to look at the story from another perspective. As in all things, distance is the writer's friend.

After the week has passed, remove the manuscript from the drawer, put it on your desk facedown, close your eyes, and run the following thought experiment.

The story as written is about your protagonist (call him Zack for now, because why not?), told largely from his perspective as he does battle against his nemesis, Devon. Zack has goals, dreams, and reasons for what he does. Zack is not just at the center of the story, Zack is the *hero* of the story.

Now turn that around: What if your protagonist was *Devon*, and the story was told from his point of view? What if he's the one who is pursuing his dreams and goals, and is being opposed by Zack, who by this interpretation becomes the story's antagonist? What would that look like? What if Devon is not just at the center of the story, but the *hero* of the story?

Because from Devon's point of view, *that's exactly what he is*.

Live with that idea for a while. Really give in to it. See it in your head.

Then, when you're ready, turn the manuscript over and—without necessarily changing the *structure* of the story, because that would mean literally starting over—revise it to put Devon psychologically at the center of every scene in which he appears. In this version of the story, *his* version, he's the hero and the driving force behind those scenes. Don't worry about the manuscript as a whole, or about going too far; just revise scene by scene while letting the structure keep you grounded and moving in the right direction.

To illustrate by example: one of the key antagonists in my series *Babylon 5* was Mr. Bester, a law enforcement officer for an organization of telepaths called the Psi Corps. Interested only in advancing the cause of his people, he has a deep distrust of non-telepaths (who he refers to as "mundanes"), which makes him a constant thorn in the side of our heroes, and over the course of the series he does some pretty awful things to them.

Whenever I finished writing a script in which Bester appeared, I would turn my hat around and revise his scenes to ensure that no matter what others said or thought about him, he always saw himself as a good man doing unfortunate things for honorable reasons. After doing this for a couple of seasons, it occurred to me: Instead of going scene by scene, what if I wrote an entire *episode* from Bester's point of view? What if instead of a TV series about *Babylon 5*, our show was *actually* about the Psi Corps? What if they were the heroes of our story, and the *Babylon 5* characters were the antagonists, constantly interfering in Bester's attempts to do the right thing by his fellow telepaths?

The result was an episode entitled "The Corps Is Mother, the Corps Is Father." I even created an entirely new title sequence that featured Bester and the Psi Corps as the focus of our series and the heroes of our story. The audience loved it, and many of them thought that it could have been a nifty little show on its own terms.

Obviously, one needn't go quite this far in turning one's hat around for the bad guy to have a degree of three-dimensionality; the point is the thought experiment behind it. The more your antagonist's motives can appear reasonable, or at least understandable enough for the audience to sympathize with them, something magical happens: the audience finds itself conflicted. They want the Good Guy to succeed because he's the Good Guy and they like him, but they also kind of get where the Bad Guy is coming from; they like him, too, at least a little, so maybe it wouldn't be *entirely* bad if he succeeded. In *The Silence of the Lambs*, Clarice needs to find the serial killer who has kidnapped a senator's daughter, and we want her to triumph over the bad guy. We also agree with her assessment that Hannibal Lecter needs to stay in prison . . . but despite all that, a part of us is quietly rooting for him, so when he gets away at the end, it's a triumph. It shouldn't be, but it is.

The need for an audience to empathize with and feel for the story's hero is obvious and can be done fairly easily. Getting the audience to feel for the bad guy is much more difficult, but once achieved, elevates the story beyond what the audience was expecting when they bought the book or the movie ticket.

TO THE UNIVERSITY OR COLLEGE STUDENT

Many beginning writers discover a passion for words during their college years, a time that presents new challenges and opportunities. Since this is a very formative time in a writer's life, I wanted to take a few moments to discuss the subject at length.

The most obvious question facing most such students—*Should I major in writing?*—is one for which there is simply no good answer beyond, *It depends*. Most of those who decide to major in Creative Writing end up as teachers instead of writers, so if that's the plan, then yes, proceed.

The choice is a little different when it comes to attending film school in pursuit of a degree in screenwriting or filmmaking. Such institutions not only provide academic training, they also serve as vocational schools, providing more in the way of contacts, training, practical resources, and hands-on experience than is generally the case with creative writing programs. Film school students pursuing an MFA in screenwriting, directing, producing, or filmmaking usually graduate after producing a variety of short films and videos that add to their viability in the marketplace.

By contrast, mainstream college and university writing programs tend to eschew the value of acquiring actual experience with production or publication, emphasizing the theoretical over the practical. Their approach to instruction is often more about how to organize and present information than about actual *storytelling* because the former is formulaic and straightforward to teach; the latter is elusive, difficult to quantify, and different for everyone who attempts it. It's easy to say, almost from rote, *Writing begins with an Introductory Paragraph, or Thesis Statement. This puts forth the point you wish to make. This is then followed by as many Body Paragraphs as are necessary to provide evidence and support for your thesis. Finally, the Concluding Paragraph restates your thesis, collates and reinforces how the preceding paragraphs provide evidence that your thesis is valid.*

Fine. Now, using that formula, show me which words, in what order, will tell a reader what it felt like when the one you loved walked away for someone else.

Emotional responses to the work only occur after it's released into the world, and unfortunately many university writing programs seem to look down at the idea of writing for publication or, worse still, writing as a job of work, a way of making a living, a *profession*. This, in turn, may explain why so few instructors are actually working writers. I experienced this prejudice firsthand the semester I taught Creative Writing 101 at San Diego State University. By this time I'd had some minor success as a writer of articles and plays, but even that was enough to incline many instructors in the department to view my appointment with disapproval. None of them were working writers, and the only instructor who could boast of having a chapbook of his poetry in print maintained that status only by requiring his students to buy it at the university bookstore every semester.

On our first day of class, I told the students that if they were in search of an easy A, they'd picked the wrong room; if they stuck around they would write more than in any other class they ever took. Not since the Exodus from Egypt have so many people run for the same door at the same time.

But it wasn't just about giving out writing assignments. As much as I lectured about the writing process, I spent an equal amount of time listening, seeking out the students' opinions, and encouraging them to explore ideas they were passionate about. For many of them, it was the first time a teacher had asked what *they* thought about things rather than telling them what they *should* think, and the class soon took on an exciting, creative, freewheeling atmosphere where any question could be asked.

In addition to discussing the theory of writing, I wanted to encourage them to actually *do* something with their work. So if they published an article in the school newspaper, I would replace any one of their tests or required papers with an A; if they sold an article or short story to a legiti-mate off-campus magazine or newspaper, they would ace the entire *course*.

On the one hand, this galvanized the students; on the other, it led to my being called on the carpet by one of the departmental Elder Gods. "We are here to teach writing on a theoretical level, not a crass, commer-cial level."

"But isn't writing meant to be shared, seen, and *read*? Isn't that the whole *reason* for it? To communicate the writer's perspective?"

"Not at all. There's no reason for anyone to see it, ever. Take Emily Dickinson, for instance."

"You *do* know how that story ends, right?" I asked, and in so doing discovered that levity is not overmuch appreciated in academic circles.

Most of my students had signed up simply because they were required to take at least one class in the English department; they hadn't come in the door expecting to become writers. The idea of publishing *anything* was the furthest thing from their minds. But the offer to substitute an A grade for a published work led nearly *half* of them to publish articles or short pieces in the college newspaper, and some actually managed to sell to the local, legitimate press. Excited to discover that they had a voice and a platform, a few of them continued to write and sell their work long after leaving my class.

This did not go over well with some in the department, and I was not asked back for another term.[1]

In the years that followed, I came to understand that SDSU's dismis-sive attitude toward writing as a profession was common among university writing instructors. *We are here to teach writing on a theoretical level, not a crass, commercial level.* But such wrongheaded notions about the art versus the craft of writing are not confined just to the staff.

While attending an awards ceremony a few years ago, I was seated at a table flanked on both sides by strangers. When they learned that I

1 Full disclosure: As this book entered the final copyediting stage, I was invited by the Television, Film, and New Media Department at San Diego State University to teach a course in Advanced Script Writing for Television and Film for the Fall 2020 semester. I attempted to get a response to this from the SDSU English Department but was precluded from doing so on account of their installing a leopard in the lobby.

was there to receive one of the awards, suddenly everyone had a question about writing: How did I get into it, what did I like about it, and where do stories come from, anyway? (My answers, boiled down to their essential core, were: *I had no choice*; *everything*; and *I have absolutely no idea.*)

During a lull in the conversation, a young woman to my right who had not spoken earlier leaned in to say that she had just graduated from college with a degree in Creative Writing. "I'm so excited to finally start writing," she said.

"Did you say *start* writing?" I asked, doing my best to sound neutral.

"Well, I've written papers for class, but that's all," she said, and now there was a hint of nervousness in her voice. "My parents paid for me to go to school to become a writer, and now that I have my degree they expect me to start making a living as a writer right away."

And as the lights dimmed and the event began, a part of me silently died on her behalf, crushed beneath the weight of an encouraging smile.

Getting a degree in Creative Writing does not immediately confer on one the status of writer, and parents should not expect their newly minted graduates to begin earning money as a writer at once. It's not the same process as learning to be a doctor or an engineer, where X method always results in Y result and there's usually a paying job waiting for you on the other side of the academic experience. The occasional annoying prodigy notwithstanding, you wouldn't expect an art major to come out of college a Picasso, or for a music major to be immediately hired by the Chicago Symphony Orchestra. Writing is an art as much as it is a craft, requiring years of trial and error, so patience is required from all sides.

For this reason, it's essential to start writing original work and trying to sell it sooner rather than later. If you wait until you have your degree in hand to begin that process, for all intents and purposes you will be starting over.

Some additional observations intended for those who are still in school:

1) CHOOSING YOUR MAJOR

As noted upstream, if it's your heart's desire to major in Creative Writing, then don't let my words discourage you; do as your soul requires. But if that degree is not necessary to your long-term plans, then you might want to consider the possibility of pursuing a *complementary* major or a *backup* major.

A complementary major is a field of study that can either assist you with some aspect of your writing, or give you credibility in areas that can help establish you as a writer even when your credits are not yet significant. So if your goal is to write articles or thrillers set against a geopolitical background, a degree in political science can be a definite advantage. If you want to write plays, consider a degree in Theater Arts.

As someone who has always felt very distant from other people, I needed help getting into the minds of my characters and feeling what they were feeling, which is what led to my first degree in Psychology. I was also drawn to the idea of writing stories about people from a global perspective, hence my second degree in Sociology. Neither of these were backup majors because there was no way I could make a living from either of them unless I went for a PhD, and that was not something I wanted to pursue. I was looking for information and training, not a piece of paper to put up on the wall. (When asked about my academic training, I usually respond by saying that the best thing about getting BA degrees in Psychology and Sociology is that "I'm qualified to be unemployed in two different directions at the same time.")

A backup major is a field of study that will help you survive financially while pursuing your career as a writer. These are often vocational in nature or involve specific training for jobs that can be done without taking too much brain power away from the writing process. (The Wachowskis, creators of the Matrix movies, and with whom I collaborated on several projects, worked as carpenters during the years they spent trying to sell scripts.)[2] Other possibilities that don't involve quite as much sawing and hammering would be computer science, real estate, game design (which

---

2 During our first meeting, at a screening for the last of the Matrix films, they said that during this time they looked to my book and monthly column on scriptwriting, both for *Writer's Digest*, for information they were able to use later in selling their first scripts. It's something I've heard repeatedly over the years from other writers, and a source of deep personal pride.

could also be viewed as a complementary major), pharmacy, mathematics, or marketing.

However: when considering a backup major, be wary of those who would use this to deflect your interest in writing rather than seeing it as a way to support yourself during those difficult early years. *You should get a job in real estate or chemistry so there's a Plan B you can fall back on in case you don't make it as a writer.* Realistically, we all know that a career in writing may not manifest itself, but the Plan B approach can often result in self-sabotage. If there's something else you *can* do for a living, the odds are that you'll end up doing exactly that in the end, because whatever it is will probably be easier than writing. If the air turns turbulent and there's a parachute in the plane, it's tempting to bail out rather than try to see the journey through. But if there *is* no parachute—or you can successfully make yourself *believe* it's not there—then you have no choice but to keep going until you come out the other side.

If you are not truly dedicated to doing what it takes to become a writer, there's no shame in using the Plan B parachute. But if you know in your heart that nothing else will suffice, then plant your feet, turn your face to the wind, and do what's necessary to bring this beast in for a landing.

2) USE YOUR RESOURCES WELL

If your college experience consists mainly of the classrooms, the commissary, and the parking lot, you're missing the point. Most college and university campuses have at least some resources that can be used to further a writer's development. These include campus newspapers and magazines, film and theater departments in need of material for students to perform or produce, podcasts, as well as television and radio stations, as well as social media content that may be based on-campus or otherwise affiliated with the university. These opportunities are important because there's something extremely validating about seeing one's name in print or on-screen for the first time, even in something as minor as a college playbill or an article in the student newspaper.

Reach out to the department heads. Not only are they accessible to student writers, in many cases they are strongly encouraged to seek out work by students in order to create cross-departmental integration and justify the cost of their specific divisions. In *Becoming Superman*, I describe the frustration among the editors at my college newspaper, the *Daily Aztec*, as they struggled to fill each day's required number of pages. The problem they faced was that talented student writers rarely thought to submit to the *DA* (presumably they believed it was a closed shop, or because its proximity made it almost invisible in a weird, taken-for-granted kind of way), and the dimmer lights who *did* show up often failed to turn in their assignments on time or, in many cases, at all. Since the publication of that book, dozens of on-campus newspaper and magazine editors have emailed or tweeted me to say that the situation hasn't changed.

The benefits of writing for campus publications and other venues goes beyond the ego-boost involved. For starters, some student newspapers actually pay for articles; it's not a lot, but for young, hungry students every dollar helps. Having your work published also creates an opportunity to receive feedback from people who have no vested interest in being nice to you. When you deliver an article and the editor tells you that it's too long and you have one hour to cut it down to meet deadlines, you learn how to edit quickly, figuring out what elements are truly necessary for the story to work and booting the rest. Actors at a college radio station or theater, or podcast hosts or producers, will ask for lines to be made easier to say, helping you understand the difference between spoken language and what works on the written page. Writing for the campus theater, newspaper, or magazine will help you build a collection of published or produced work that can be useful in getting a paying job at a similar venue after graduation.

3) DON'T BE AFRAID

The biggest advantage to starting one's writing career while still in college is that there is less at stake if things don't immediately work out. The real world can be an unforgiving place when rent is on the line. College should be a time when nobody expects you to be perfect and it's safe to be fearless, to experiment, and make mistakes, to screw up, to fail, fall, and laugh it off and get back up and try it again.

And then there's the inoculation aspect to be considered.

Vaccines work by injecting the patient with a harmless or inert version of a virus, to which the patient develops a vigorous response, creating antibodies that can be called upon to combat a more invasive version of the live virus. Dealing with fear can be much the same for new writers. Coming fresh out of college with no prior production or publication background, the prospect of submitting one's work for the first time to newspapers, online publications, book publishers, or producers can be daunting in the extreme. But having the experience of submitting one's work to editors, directors, and filmmakers working within an academic environment takes the edge off the fear. Like a vaccine, it gives us a less threatening version of the experience so that we can face the real thing without fear.

Taking advantage of the resources available at your college will let you burn through all the marginal work, hone your talent to razor sharpness, give you a measure of courage and confidence going forward, and with luck, allow you to leave the university with dozens of credits—perhaps even some in the outside world—and a world of experience to support your quest to become a working writer.

SYSTEMS OF CREATION

I got into an argument online today and you're going to pay for it.

A guy asked what "model" I used for my writing, which "diagrams and layouts" of the writing process available in various writing texts I followed. When I asked, politely, what the hell he was talking about, he refined the question in an effort to determine what format (or guide to creating stories) I used and would thus recommend to others. Did I use the Story Diamond, for instance, or did I prefer the breakdown style that denotes what specific events should happen by equally specific page numbers (complication on page 15, reversal for the hero on page 90, etc.).

A bit more prodding led to the conclusion I'd hoped we weren't barreling toward. The question at the core of his interest, the *real* question, the question *behind* his question, was: *What's the Formula?*

I said there's no such thing.

He got miffed.

I said that the "models," diagrams, and layouts found in most writing texts serve one of two purposes: in their most well-meaning iteration they are cobbled together in an attempt to analyze the writing process *after* the fact of creation; in other, more cynical iterations, they are advanced by those hoping to brand their own style of instruction for purposes of marketing, because you can't sell something unless it's uniquely yours. *Here is my model of the writing process—this the formula, this is how it works, so if you want to be successful, your only choice is to buy my books and come to my seminars at three hundred bucks per head.*

He got even more miffed.

I suggested that some writers fall back on models[1] as a substitute for vision, voice, talent, and the courage to back them up. They want someone to tell them what to write and how to write because they have nothing of their own to say, so they're looking for the Secret Handshake that will make them Writers without having to suffer and bleed for it.

And *boy* did he get steamed. We're talking *miffus maximus*.

He accused me of withholding valuable information from up-and-coming writers because I didn't want competition. How could I possibly know how to structure my stories without some overriding methodology or formula that could provide clear, objective direction? But the comment that finally tipped me over was when he said I was misleading people out of ego; that I was making this writing thing sound like it was all about art because it allowed me to put on airs and pretend to be special; after all, the *only* way I could make a living at writing was if I made sure my work followed "market styles for trends."

He concluded that because I was a commercial writer, because I wrote for *money*, because I was *successful* at it, if I said I *didn't* follow a formula and do all those commercially smart things, well, then I was just a hack and a liar.

There is a moment in every old-school western when the new guy in town, hopped up on whiskey and misplaced confidence, rolls up on the resident gunslinger and says something unfortunate, and everybody else runs for cover because they don't want to be anywhere *near* what happens next.

Suffice to say that while his body may one day be found, it could never be identified from what's left.

The only thing more stupid than taking on a writer in a written medium is the assumption behind those questions: that there is some external formula to be downloaded, a schematic that will allow someone to insert tab A into slot B and *blammo!* there's a best-selling story or script.

Let me be clear: It. Does. Not. Exist.

Stories are not born by following someone else's rules; they are not the product of number crunching or trend analysis; they come from a

---

1 And frankly, no one should ever fall back on models because their lives are difficult enough without adding personal injury to the list.

very deep and personal place in the creative heart that needs to talk about things that matter. Yes, there is a place for inspiration, an overheard comment that triggers the storytelling process, an image that becomes a novel, a researched bit of data that creates a character that births a screenplay, but once that inspiration goes through the crazy-straw of your talent it comes out as something profoundly and uniquely your own.

And yes, it's important to know the rules of writing, but only inasmuch as they provide a safety net for experimentation, bending or breaking them as needed once we understand that stories can look like whatever we *want* them to look like. You can write beginning-middle-end in sequence . . . or start at the end, back your way into the beginning, and end on the middle (as in *Pulp Fiction* or *The Usual Suspects*) . . . or begin at the middle then flip to the beginning, sandwiching in all your story elements until you arrive at the story's conclusion (a la *Reservoir Dogs* or *All About Eve*) . . . or start at the end and work your way backward to the beginning (*Memento* and *Arrival*).

As demonstrated by writers ranging from James Joyce to William Burroughs, you can do pretty much anything you want with a story provided you can pull it off convincingly.

But what's wrong *with doing a market analysis of what's currently in bookstores or theaters to determine what's being made so we know what to write?* I hear you ask.

Absent online publication, which can happen much more speedily, all the books currently in stores, and all the films now in theaters, were purchased, put into production, commissioned, or written anywhere *from one to two years earlier*. It takes time to sell, edit, and publish a novel, or move a script through the process of being cast, prepped, shot, and distributed. When you step into a theater or a bookstore, you're walking back in time to what editors and studios were buying much earlier, and have subsequently moved on; what was fashionable then isn't fashionable now, so if you write to those examples you're already two years behind the curve of what's currently being bought.

At no point in this book will I tell you what your story should look like, when certain things should happen broken down by page count, or suggest that there is a Formula that applies in all circumstances in all genres.

I'm not trying to sell you on my Model. I believe firmly that the real, authentic process of writing is as individual as the writer him- or herself. That doesn't mean flailing around in the dark without guidance—there's plenty of that here and in other books on writing—but in the end, the only way to find real, sustained success is by finding your own process, style, and voice.

While I'm picking fights, let me go on the record as saying that I also have a problem with people who advocate for the godlike infallibility of the Three Act Structure in films. This may seem like the worst kind of heresy but hear me out. Film school instructors often go to great lengths to explain that when New York playwrights moved west during the early years of motion pictures, they brought with them the three-act structure used in theater. Well, yeah, because it was the chief paradigm they had to work with at the time. If the only tool you have is a hammer, every problem is a nail. It also ignores a crucial point that never seems to come up in film class.

The reason these playwrights hewed to a three-act structure was that live theaters needed intermissions *to sell snacks and change costumes and sets.* Each act came to a crescendo, the curtain came down, people walked to the back for a candy bar or a drink or to use the restroom, then after fifteen minutes settled back into their seats as the curtain came up on a new set with the cast dressed in different wardrobe. Anyone who wants to drag the tradition of live theater into modern-day media in an attempt to justify the three-act structure needs to be reminded that Shakespeare wrote in five acts, and Greek plays were generally just *one* act because snacks were sold during the play, and there was no need to change sets or costumes since robes were all the rage and practical sets were rarely used.

If academics are serious about using the three-act structure in film, then they should go all the way with their premise and insist that theaters stop the movie every forty minutes for an intermission. But they don't, and they won't, because they know that audiences would react to such chicanery by storming the box office armed with torches, pitchforks, and at least one copy of the *Watchtower.* Further, the baseline definition of multiple-act structure requires that each act builds slowly to a big moment of action or revelation at the end of the act, which hooks the audience into sticking around after the intermission. But no one expects a contemporary movie audience to wait thirty to forty minutes for a Big Moment; depending on genre, those moments tend to happen every ten to fifteen minutes.

Bladders permitting, audiences in movie theaters watch the entire story from beginning to end in one throw, so from their perspective it's all just one long act. Which is why many filmmakers in recent years have started writing their stories as a single act that starts at frame one and doesn't let up until the end credits roll. Films such as the Jason Bourne series are preeminent examples of one-act wonders. Other filmmakers have chosen to kick the three-act structure to the curb in favor of writing even *more* acts divided up by the intent of their story. *All That Jazz* arguably works over five acts; *Magnolia, Memento, Inception*, and *The Usual Suspects* couldn't care less about act structure; and Quentin Tarantino has made a career out of poking his finger in the eye of traditional three-act structure, in one example literally numbering his five acts (or chapters) in both *Kill Bill* films as they sailed past the "accepted" limit.

Breaking down movies into three acts, and novels into their traditional five-part structure (introduction, rising action, complication, climax, and denouement), is best suited as a tool for the *analysis* of storytelling rather than the actual process of creation. It is also useful for writers when working with editors and executives who still hew to those structures. When I get an assignment that requires drafting an outline as step one, I write the story straight through, end to end, no act breaks. I make it as tight as I can while ensuring that the characters and the scenes pop emotionally, because *those* are the things that the reader wants to see. Then I count the number of pages, divide by three, and label the acts accordingly. If I've done my job right, and every scene ends strongly, then *any* scene and *every* scene can serve equally well as an act-out.

And I've *never* had an executive say that the act breaks fell in the wrong places.

Having begun this tirade talking about writing systems, let me try to explain the steps I use when developing a story. It's idiosyncratic and may not work for everyone, but at least it won't cost you three hundred dollars a day.

I start out with a fresh notepad[2] that is only for this one project, and begin filling it with notes on characters, plot elements, and in particular, any scenes I can already see in my head that make sense within the context of the story I want to tell. (I have plenty of outlining and word-processing systems, but when in the early creative stages I prefer to handwrite everything because it slows me down, forcing me to think through each scene in detail. Also, using pen-and-paper makes everything feel less final and more malleable than when it's been typed onto the screen, but if you want to do this on a laptop I'm not going to come to your house and argue about it.)[3] I don't put a time limit on the process or decide in advance how much material I need, and I don't worry about sequence. Page 6 of the notepad might have a good scene from the first part of the work, and page 7 might have something I can use at the very end. It's about being fluid and flexible, allowing the mind to be playful while the story accretes naturally, jotting down bits and pieces as they emerge from the woolgathering process. Before calling it a night, I put the notepad on the bedside table in case any midnight revelations come looking for me.

When I've gone as far as I can with the story at this stage, I transfer everything to 3x5 cards, one card per scene, with separate cards for background information about characters and setting. Once all the scenes have been written out on cards, I put them in chronological order and start going through them, watching the movie or novel unspool in front of me. If two scenes feel too similar, I ditch whichever is weakest, and add transitional scenes as needed. *They found a body on the floor in scene 15, so I'll probably need a scene 15a that shows the coroners arriving to give us necessary information about the murder, or if I want to hold that back for a while, we should at least see the body being driven off.* I try to be ruthless in attacking the story structure and the motivations of my characters; whatever can go should go, what can be

---

2 For those who are deeply into the "what sort of notepad do you use?" paper fetish—and I confess to being one of them—I use the Freeleaf Annotation Ruled Pads from Levenger because they have a nice, narrow-ruled page, which takes fountain pen ink well, but best of all, they have a window on the left-hand side that runs the length of the page, which lets me annotate material and add notes during the process or much later without having to try to fit them inside the lines. It allows me to think both linearly and nonlinearly at the same time.
3 Unless you like that sort of thing, in which case leave your details with my agent.

improved should be, and only the absolutely necessary is allowed to stick around. (See "Questions of Intent" for more on this.)

When I've finished revising the cards in the current order, I take one last run at it to attack the structure. The great thing about 3x5 cards, and the reason I recommend them, is that they're easily moved around. *What if I move this scene back later in the story as a flashback? What if I move this scene forward as foreshadowing? How would it play if I started in the middle, or at the end?* Have *fun* with the story, and see what it looks like in different permutations. Be playful in ways that will encourage the creative part of your brain to explore options that you may never have considered while telling the story linearly.

Sometimes I'll start with thirty scene cards and end up with eighty; other times I'll start with one hundred cards and end up with seventy. The number changes again once the actual writing begins, revealing more scenes that can be tossed out or that need to be inserted, allowing the story to grow organically in unexpected directions. Rather than trying to control everything, I try to live in the moment with each character in each scene, letting them, and the story, breathe. It's one thing to guess what the characters *might* do in a given situation, and another matter entirely when you're living with them during the writing process and seeing what they *actually* do in that moment.

It's important to know where you're going while remaining open to surprises, because as noted elsewhere in this book, surprises are essential to good storytelling; if you can't surprise yourself, you can never surprise an audience. It's like deciding to take a vacation drive from San Francisco to San Diego: you know where you're starting and where you plan to end, and some of the stops you want to make along the way, but you allow yourself the opportunity to get off the main road from time to time to see what unexpected delights might be found along the way.

The foregoing development process may work for some of you and may drive others mad. And that's okay. Writing methods are like dietary habits; what works for some of you would almost certainly kill me, and vice versa. So if those suggestions are too methodical, feel free to boot them down the stairs. Some writers like to start with just an idea and plunge directly into the writing, letting the story reveal itself to them as a process of discovery rather than planning. And to be honest, there have been times when I've had no choice but to go the discovery route.

Example the First: A while back, I was called in to rewrite a movie for Warner Bros. Prior to the meeting, I knew nothing about the project, not even the title (*Ninja Assassin*). During our discussion, they explained that this was to be a complete, page-one rewrite, fade in to fade out; essentially, a whole new script. Even more daunting, they wanted the draft to be delivered by that Friday morning in order to get it out to talent agents. The meeting took place on a Tuesday afternoon. Allowing for an hour or two of sleep here and there, the math said that I would have about fifty-two hours to write an entirely new draft, end to end.

I went home, fired up the coffee machine, and just started writing. No cards, no plan, *ready-steady-go!* Not only was the script turned in on deadline that Friday morning, it received no notes from the studio. That's not how I generally work, but the challenge was fun, and I had the thrill of learning how to use my legs all over again when I finally stood up from my desk.

Example the Second: Not long after my film *Changeling* picked up some Oscar nominations and a BAFTA nomination for Best Screenplay, I was called in for a meeting at Universal with Steven Spielberg and Stacey Snider, who was then CEO of DreamWorks. They explained that there was a passion project that Steven had been trying to get written for years but could never get a draft that met his expectations of what the story could be. (And no, I'm not going to tell you what it is because keeping that secret was part of the deal.)

As they described the nature of the project, I immediately understood why there were problems; the subject matter had been explored many times before, but never very well. The more we talked, the more I began to realize that the only way to tell this story would be to adopt a more experimental form of writing than I was known for, or had ever attempted previously. So when they were finished, I said that, yes, I believed I could do it, but that I would not be able to give them an outline or even a sense of how I would write the script. I would have to research and dig and study every aspect of this particular story until I could finally hear the voice of the main character in my head. Once that happened, I would have to dive right into the script without pause until I hit FADE OUT.

In short, they'd have to trust me and I'd have to trust an aspect of my process that I'd never dared to try before.

They shared an uncertain look, then Steven finally nodded. "That's not how we usually work, but because it's you, if you really think you can pull this off, then go and do."

I spent the next six months researching the story, traveling around Los Angeles, and sifting through articles, archives, and newspaper morgues, and interviewing people. But the storyteller voice at the back of my head remained silent. I kept digging, desperately feeding the Muse in the hope that somehow, something would come of it.

Then, one night, just as I was falling asleep . . . I heard the main character's voice in my head. Just talking. Just *being*. I kicked off the sheets, ran into the office at the back of my house, and started writing. I know for a fact that I didn't sleep the first day, and got maybe an hour or two here and there over the next few days. I didn't return calls or leave the house. The story had me in its teeth and wouldn't let go.

Exactly fourteen days after the writing began, I hit the end, then slept for twenty-four hours. When I was conscious again, I looked through the draft. It worked. It was solid. Not because of anything I'd done, but because of the authenticity of the voice at its center; the story had done all the hard work telling itself—I was just the guy typing it up. I fixed some typos, then sent it in that day as it was, without revision.

Several days passed. I began to worry that I'd screwed it up, that maybe I should have taken some time to revise it or reconsider some of the story. But at my core I knew that the story was only and exactly what it needed to be. *You heard that voice*, a small voice in the back of my head whispered. *Now trust that voice.*

A day later, the phone rang. A woman's voice said, "Please hold for Steven Spielberg."

There's no way to describe the ten thousand ways that sentence can twist a writer's stomach into knots of hope and apprehension. Then there was a click and Steven's voice came onto the line.

"You knocked it out of the park," he said.

I cannot discuss the project further for the reasons already given, but I can tell you that it may well be the best thing I've ever written, or ever will write. Because Steven and Stacey trusted me, and because I was willing to listen to the voice of the story.[4]

Both methods—planning the story and letting the story happen to you—can work equally well, depending on the story you want to tell. I tend to favor the former because looking into the abyss comes at a price that I am not always willing to endure.

Figuring out which method of story development works best for you comes only with time, practice, and self-discovery. There's no one-size-fits-all solution that works for everyone all the time. Keep going until you find something that fits and looks cool. Trust yourself and your instincts. Follow the path that feels right, and in most cases, it will be right, for you.

---

4 After delivering the script, Steven had to take several long-term film projects in the action/science fiction category to fulfill contractual obligations, so as I write this it sits on a shelf at Amblin awaiting the right window, which can take many years. Clint Eastwood held on to the script for *Unforgiven* for eight years before filming. Regardless: of all the screenplays I've written, this is my favorite.

MAKING TIME

As noted elsewhere, the more pages you write, the more stories you finish, the better you will get, acquiring new tools and building up a library of material that you can begin to sell. But finding windows of opportunity to push out those pages can sometimes be difficult. People have jobs and families and social obligations and a host of other distractions, necessary or trivial, that can get in the way of the work.

I'd love to get more done, but I can't find the time.

If being a writer matters to you, then you don't *find* the time, you *make* the time.

Step One is to be clear in your own head about what you're attempting. New writers, along with their friends and families, often view these early efforts as a hobby, something you do when you're not working at an actual *job*. But writing is not a hobby—it's a profession no different than being a plumber, a teacher, or a doctor, and if you don't treat it seriously, nobody else will do so. Whenever you plant yourself behind the keyboard or the notepad, that time should feel as necessary and important as showing up at medical school, or carpentry class, or a construction company.

A while back, I was invited by several friends to a small dinner, and arrived to find someone who I knew aspired to be a writer also in attendance. "How's the writing going?" I asked.

"I'm working on the writing," he said.

"I'm not entirely sure what 'working on the writing' means," I said. "Are you actually *writing* or just *thinking* about writing?"

As the other guests looked on awkwardly (this probably explains why I don't get many dinner invitations), he twisted and turned, ducked and dodged, feathered and faltered, backed and filled and looked out the window (the foregoing technique is called *cataloging*) in the desperate hope that a passing UFO might divert the conversation. When none appeared, he finally admitted that he hadn't written anything in months. "But I'm *thinking* about it," he said.

Consider that comment in another context.

"You said you were training for the Olympics—how's that going?"

"I'm working on the training."

"But are you actually *training*?"

"No, I haven't trained in months, but I'm *thinking* about it."

An athlete doesn't just train the night before the big game. S/he does the work every day, making it a habit as regular as breathing. You get it *done*, period. This means actually *writing*, not sitting at a coffee shop with your laptop open to the same page you've been staring at for the last month, waiting for someone to see what's on the screen and say, "So, are you a writer?"

(You know who you are. Knock it off.)

Step Two: Set reasonable and achievable goals. Decide what you want to write during the next twelve months—a novel? screenplay? three short stories?—then do the math. The average novel weighs in at about 100,000 words, which equals 285 words per day. That's just a tick over one page. Hardly that scary, is it? As John Steinbeck said, "When I face the desolate impossibility of writing five hundred pages, a sick sense of failure falls on me, and I know I can never do it. Then gradually, I write one page and then another. One day's work is all I can permit myself to contemplate."

One page per day for a year is three screenplays, seven TV scripts, or eighteen short stories per year. If that's still too daunting, you can write one movie or three short stories per year by knocking down just one-third of a page, or about sixty words, per day. Don't think about climbing the mountain, just keep putting one foot in front of the other until you run *out* of mountain. If you miss a day, don't try to make up for it the next day by writing twice as much, because you might not hit that number and now you'll feel like you're falling even *further* behind and the anxiety over getting it done will increase exponentially.

If necessary, get up an hour early, while the house/apartment/dorm is quiet, or stay up later at night, when everyone's asleep, and make that your time to write undisturbed. That last word is desperately important. If there are other people around while you're writing, you *have* to make them understand that, yes, you're just in the next room, but for all intents and purposes you're on Mars and not to be interrupted.

Try to make your appointment with the keyboard at the same time, and in the same place, every day. Studies in state-related learning have shown that if you teach a group of students a given subject in Classroom A, then divide them into two groups and test them on that subject, with half in Classroom A and half in Classroom B, the students who take the test in Classroom A will almost always do better than the others. Being tested in the same place where they learned the information provided visual, spatial, and emotional cues that helped them recall it later. Similarly, making an effort to write in the same room, at the same time, makes it easier for your brain to reconnect with what you were doing the day before. This can jump-start the process so you're not wasting valuable time.

Step Three: Once you have your attitude in gear, with a time and place in which to write for an hour, you have to make the most of every second. Use as much of your time after the prior day's writing to plan out what you intend to write, rolling it around in your head until you have the first bits worked out, so you can hit the ground running. Once you reach the end of what you planned out, the odds are good that more of the story will have shown up and you can keep going. (For more advice on how to make the most of your time see "Muse-Ings.") Don't use this time to revise; you can always edit later, once everything's down on paper. You can't revise what's not there, so just focus on getting down as many new words as possible.

Once you've hit the end of the hour or the day's minimum word count, you can stop with a clear conscience. If the words are still coming fast and furious, keep going for as long as you remain undisturbed, but continuing today doesn't mean you get to take tomorrow off; you still have to do your minimum number of words the next day. Don't turn this into a bargaining process. Stick to the routine. As your confidence grows, you can try incrementally increasing your word count. Going from one to two pages per day is a triumph to be celebrated.

The more you write, the more things you can sell; the more you can sell, the more money you make; and the more money you make, the more time you have for your art.

Don't work on the writing. *Write.*

Don't try to find the time. *Make* the time.

And sit up straight. You're slouching.

Again.

VALUE ADDED

A brief benediction before closing out this section.

Almost all of us collect something. Purses or ties, laptops or cell phones, hotel keys or mugs or T-shirts or sports banners or broken hearts or concert tickets (or, in the case of writers, tons and tons of rejection slips) . . . I collect fountain pens. For a long time I had just two, but then I made the mistake of buying a third, and once you have three of anything you're a collector, so now I have close to a hundred. I love the colors, their design and shapes, the heft when you pick them up, and the way they deliver ink to the page. Most of them are relatively inexpensive, twenty or thirty bucks, others cost a few hundred dollars, and there are some I don't want to talk about because I should never have spent that kind of money on freaking pens but damn they're beautiful. At the moment, my favorite fountain pen is the Pilot Custom 823, recommended by friend and fellow writer Neil Gaiman, because it's an absolute workhorse, has a cool locking mechanism to keep the pen from going dry, and holds a ton of ink.

I collect them because I appreciate craftsmanship and beauty. (It's almost certainly not coincidental that my fountain pen fetish shifted into high gear around the same time that my work became about the pursuit of beauty in writing.) I like the smooth flow of the ink, the ritual of having to fill and clean the pen, and knowing that the nibs gradually bend to the way you hold the pen, becoming uniquely yours. But what I like most about them is that they connect me to the history of writing. To use a fountain pen is to feel linked to all those who preceded me, reminding on a daily basis that writing is an art, a noble profession, and a holy chore.

Earlier in this book, I quoted Irving Thalberg, who said, "Writers are the most important people in Hollywood, but we must never tell the sons of bitches." Sadly, he is not alone in that appraisal. Writers are often dismissed or derided by critics who focus on the contributions of the director to the near-exclusion of all else, and by large chunks of society who rarely take aspiring writers seriously. Tell someone you've just met at a bar that you're a writer and they'll reach for a stiffer drink every time.

During the years it takes for a writer to become established, they are subjected to skepticism and doubt, their dreams written off as outbursts of unwarranted ego, and their prospects of success considered unlikely at best or impossible at worst. Which is why, of all the qualities a writer must master in the early years, endurance is the most important. For many, the process is like putting one's hand in a bucket of bees and holding it there, year after year, until people finally take you seriously.

So when some snicker or shrug dismissively when you say, *I'm a writer*, remember this:

Writers change the world.

Writers contextualize the past, interrogate the present, and create the future, *all at the same time*.

Every inch of human progress begins with an idea, with *words*, and the ability to express them in ways that will draw others together in common cause, inspiring constitutions and treatises and revolutions and cultural transformations. Whether you are an aspiring or an established writer, you stand in a procession of storytellers that stretches back to the first human to look beyond the edge of the cave and speculate about what might be moving out there in the shadows. Your lineage includes Hemingway and Shakespeare and Twain and Jane Austen, Kafka and Dumas, Dante and Dickinson, Chaucer and Brontë and Sophocles. If asked who they are and what they do, each would reply, without hesitation, *I am a writer*.

Just as *you* are a writer.

And like them, you are engaged in important, noble work.

Empathy is the baseline requirement for civilization. Primitive societies had empathy for their own tribe, while perceiving the tribe across the river as frightening, as the *enemy*. Then they met the tribe across the river and decided they weren't so bad after all, and were included in their empathy, while the people farther away on the other side of the hill became the enemy.

As empathy spreads, civilization spreads.

As empathy contracts, civilization contracts.

And writers are stewards of empathy. When we are at our best, writing uplifts, enriches, and ennobles. We put the reader into the mind of people they've never met, from different classes, castes, and ethnicities, and create empathy for those who may seem profoundly different than the audience. We make the reader *care* for that person and hope that they will succeed despite innumerable obstacles. For that reason, writers and artists have always been, and will always *be*, targeted by those who profit most from our divisions.

Writers are not hacks, replaceable and interchangeable, a dime a dozen.

Writers are explorers, charting the longitude and latitude of the human heart.

Writers are architects, building cathedrals out of words that will outlast entire civilizations. The Roman Empire is gone, but Virgil remains. The Third Reich, backed up by the mightiest war machine in human history, lies shattered in the dustbin of history, but the soft words of Anne Frank persist.

Writers are time travelers, pointing to the past, to say *this is where we came from,* and to the future, to say *this is where we are going and what we should aspire to become*, while still very much living in the present, to ask *who are we, and how shall we honor those who came before us to pave the way for our inheritors yet to come?*

That legacy of centuries runs through every writer's blood and should be celebrated every day, in ways big and small. When I see ink stains on my fingers from my fountain pen, I remember that Yeats and Virginia Woolf stared at similar markings, the writer's fingertip tattoo; it makes me proud and keeps me humble.

Every time you sit down to write, you are creating art and beauty, telling stories about our magnificent and deeply flawed humanity that, with luck and endurance, will be read and quoted hundreds of years from now.

There is honor, nobility, and grace in what you do.

Never let the world make you forget that.

STAYING
A WRITER

WHO ARE YOU?

VERSION 2.0

Congratulations! After years of struggle and heartache, you've begun selling your work to film studios and/or television and/or magazines and/or book publishers. You've answered the most important question facing any writer: Can you make a living selling your work? And the answer is yes! So *now* what do you do?

The answer is to keep challenging yourself as a writer and an artist, pushing your abilities to the maximum by aiming higher and writing better. The early struggles were nothing compared to what's now about to come your way. Anyone can start the race; only a few have the strength to go the distance.

Maybe you're a writer of prose fiction whose first novel has finally been published, and the dreaded Sophomore Blues have reared their hydra-like head to slow your progress on book number two.

Maybe you've had some modest financial success but are looking for ways to maximize your revenue and achieve the stability needed to create what you *want* to create, rather than what you *have* to create to pay the bills.

Maybe you've sold a few freelance TV scripts and you'd like to move up to a staff job, or branch out into writing movies.

Maybe you've had a solid career as a writer for some time, but the assignments are starting to slow down because your work has lost the element of surprise, and you're looking to reinvent yourself as an artist.

Maybe you've spent so much time working in one particular form or genre that you can feel the work becoming stale; or you're being given stupid notes and don't know how to deal with them; or you're eager to learn new techniques that will take you from where you *are* as a writer to where you want to *be*; or you want to try collaborating with other writers.

Or maybe you're a little lost, because once you're in the tall grass of a profession as uncertain as writing, it's easy to lose your way personally, professionally, and creatively.

If so, know that you are not alone. We all endure that struggle.

Read on.

NOTA BENE

The downside of making a living as a writer is that you're selling stories to other humans, and sometimes humans have peculiar ideas on how to improve your work. We call these notes. They're sometimes helpful, sometimes not, and on occasion they're so stupid that even a stray cat, overhearing the conversation, would spontaneously develop the power of speech *just* so it could say to the note-giver in question, "What the hell is *wrong* with you?" before running off in pursuit of a cricket or a three-movie deal at Disney.

The question, then, is how to deal with notes *constructively*, without giving offense or appearing difficult, but also without compromising your artistic vision.

Writers tend to believe our work is sacrosanct, that it doesn't need improvement. If we're lucky, we continue to believe that for a few weeks after the work is finished, but sooner or later we will reread what we wrote and see only the blemishes, the illogics, and the things we'd do differently, all the flaws that only become apparent when we have enough distance from the act of creation to do that. So it would be nice to believe that someone else could view our work objectively and save us from ourselves, but that is rarely the case. Everyone comes to the work from a position of subjectivity. Responding to a critic, Georg Christoph Lichtenberg once wrote, "A book is like a mirror. If an ass peers in, you can't expect an apostle to peer out." Just because someone is *not* you doesn't automatically make them *smarter* than you or more entitled to an opinion about your process, your methods, or your story.

But that being said, I've worked with many editors, executives, and producers who knew how to compensate for their subjectivity and were able to perceive flaws in my work that were completely invisible to me. Having not been involved in its creation, their egos weren't on the line, and that distinction can be extremely helpful. Writers live so deep inside the fishbowl of our own perceptions that we often can't see what's obvious to everyone else.

So the first step in addressing notes is to determine whether one is dealing with the aforementioned ass or an apostle. If the reader is someone you respect—a gifted writer, an executive who has shown acumen in dealing with others, or a friend or family member who is willing to be honest about your work even at the risk of pissing you off—then you should approach the process with good intentions and guarded optimism.

It's easy to recognize a smart note because it sounds a lot like the examples of constructive criticism offered in the chapter "Writing for the Workshop." An insightful critique can reveal ideas you may have had in your head during the writing process but which, for whatever reason, never made it into the draft. If the beginning is too slow, you may be asked to tighten it up; if too fast, then you may need to give the characters more room to breathe. A smart note addresses holes in story logic, technologies that don't actually work the way you want them to work, factual errors, convenient coincidences in place of rigorous plotting, and inconsistencies in character (such as a coward acting heroically without transitional moments that could justify the change, because character development is a process, not a light switch).

When a story is published or a script gets produced, the audience has no way of knowing who came up with what. A good idea is a good idea, and if it makes your story better, you get to bask in the reflected glow of someone else's wisdom and no one need ever be the wiser. Getting good notes, *smart* notes, is a wonderful thing.

Stupid notes, not so much. When those come, it's your responsibility to decide what you do or don't agree with and take a stand accordingly. Never let someone in authority pressure you into making changes that ring false for your characters or your story. That person isn't you, and while their criticisms may sound well-reasoned, they will never *truly* understand the subtler points of what you are trying to communicate because they exist outside your paradigm. Saying this may annoy some editors or executives, but notes are sometimes wrongheaded, born out of ignorance, ego, blind adherence to a formula, or a fundamental failure to understand what the story is attempting to achieve.

While working on *The Twilight Zone* for MGM and CBS, I story-edited a script by an outside writer based on Tom Godwin's short story "The Cold Equations." The story concerns an emergency-dispatch ship sent from one colony world to save another that is on the verge of being wiped out by disease. To maximize speed and fuel efficiency, the ship is stripped of every ounce of disposable weight. Even with a full "tank," the ship has just enough fuel for the pilot and the desperately needed medical supplies, not an ounce more.

Once the ship is en route to the colony, the pilot discovers a stowaway: the sixteen-year-old sister of one of the men he has been sent to save. She slipped aboard hoping to see her brother and make sure he's okay, little understanding the horrific position in which she has now put herself. If they keep going, her added weight means they won't have enough fuel to land; the ship will crash and the colonists, including her brother, will die. If they turn back, they'll miss the window for the medical supplies and, again, everyone on the colony will die.

The pilot does as much as he can to extend their available fuel, ditching every last bit of expendable equipment, but it's not enough. The only way the ship can reach its destination and save the hundreds of colonists is if one of them walks out the airlock. It can't be the pilot, because he's the only one who knows how to fly this thing. It has to be the sister. Tearful, wracked by the terror of knowing what she has to do, she sacrifices her life to save her brother and the other colonists.

So yeah, not exactly light comedy. The story's strict adherence to the immutable laws of physics, that X-amount of fuel will get Y-people Z-distance but no farther, is what made "The Cold Equations" a highly regarded story in the annals of science fiction. But MGM hated it. They said the ending was "a downer" and insisted that it be changed. "The pilot just figures it out, that's all—why is this such a big deal?" one of the execs said on a conference call, rather loudly. "We see that it's touch-and-go, we're not sure they're going to make it, but at the last minute he pulls it out and they land safely and the girl is reunited with her brother."

"Okay, but *how?*" I asked. "The math is the math is the math."

"Nobody's going to care!"

"*I* care," I said. "So will everybody who knows this story and wants to see it adapted correctly."

Every few days, more notes arrived suggesting different solutions, none of which made any kind of logical sense, so I kept saying no. Eliminate that tearful ending, take the science out of the science fiction, and there's nothing left. The more I said no, the harder the executive pushed back, the more memos were sent, and the hotter the conversations became. Under other circumstances, he probably would've just spiked the script, but by this point we'd burned through our budget for scripts, and MGM was not going to give us a penny more. They wanted *this* script with a *happy* ending, not the *scary* ending, and that was *that*.

Executive producer Mark Shelmerdine (the same producer who agreed to buy "The Hellgrammite Method" mentioned elsewhere in this volume) had always been a fierce champion of my work and often stood guard between me and the studio, but after a while even he wavered a little. "Maybe we should give him what he wants. After all, it's just one script."

I dug in even harder.

Finally came the exec's last salvo, a memo in which he laid out what he believed was an airtight solution to the problem. Paraphrased from memory (but that memory is extremely vivid), the memo said: "We leave everything just as it is in the first half of the story so it looks like the only way out is for her to leave the ship, right up to the moment when she decides to walk out the airlock, but we don't see it happen. Then we see the ship landing, the door opens, and there's the girl, alive and safe. She runs out into the arms of her brother. Then we see the pilot and discover that he's cut off both his legs and jettisoned them to make up the weight difference."

If there is a pantheon of foolish notes, that last sentence sits at the very tippy-top of the pyramid. So I said no *and* made it clear that if they insisted on gutting the story, I would have to quit the show. I didn't want to do it, but there are times when putting your skin on the line is the only way to get what you believe is the right story out into the world. We didn't hear anything for several days, by which point I was pretty sure I'd have to leave. But at the eleventh hour the executive relented, the script went into production as written, and it became one of the most memorable episodes from that season.

If a stupid note comes from someone with no power over you or your work, it's easy to say no and keep telling your story, your way. But if the stupid note comes from someone who *does* have power over you or your work, and you strongly disagree with it, the appropriate response . . . . is exactly the same.

When I lecture about this, invariably someone in the audience will say, "Well, sure, it's easy for you to say no at this point in your career, but what about beginners or writers who're still making their way up the ladder? We don't have that same power."

Actually, you do, and it's important to start exercising that power from the very beginning, even if pain is the result. Compromises are like snakes; the moment you let even one of them get past you they start multiplying. After all, if you compromised over *there* when the stakes were much smaller, why not do the same over *here* where there's more at risk? Cowardice is cumulative. So is courage. The sooner you learn to take a stand and stick to it, the easier the process becomes, until you no longer have to debate or fret over the choice—it's pure reflex, as natural as breathing.

Here's the crux of it for every writer of any ability, at any point in his or her career.

If you have your integrity, nothing else matters.

If you don't have your integrity, nothing else matters.

To be clear: *Never compromise* is not synonymous with not being collaborative. If a compromise will *improve* the work, then go for it. Reaching for a tactical nuclear weapon should never be your first response. In the case of "The Cold Equations," I tried repeatedly and at length to reason with the executive before entering the launch codes. Whenever there's been a conflict between myself and an executive, editor, or publisher, I enter Thunderdome under very specific rules of engagement: *I agree not to pull a diva routine on you, and you agree not to pull rank; we will stay in the room and talk it out until I genuinely convince you, or you genuinely convince me, of the rightness of our respective views.* In this case the executive's *Take it or leave it* approach required a DEFCON 1 response, but most of the time the result can be simpler, more productive, or finessed. Often it comes down to simply realizing that *this* executive gave you *that* note because he wants to feel that he's been *heard*, that he's a valued part of the process.

And there are a million ways to fox such individuals.

One way is to simply let time pass. Often the note-giver will forget the specifics of his or her suggestions by the time you turn in the next draft.

Another approach is to praise the note-giver and humble yourself. *I loved the note; I thought it was a great idea, so I tried every way I could think of to make it work, but the way the rest of the story lays out I just couldn't pull it off.* The note-giver will be disappointed, but if they believe that you heard them and respected their input and truly gave it your best shot, they will usually relent with fond benedictions for your future career.

And sometimes, if you're really, *really* good at it, you can just lie your way out.

Let's say the note-giver suggests that instead of having your character come through the door in a given scene because it's too predictable, you should have him come through the window instead. *It'll be more dramatic and a big surprise for the audience.*

You smile and nod and write it down even though you know it won't work because the story requires the apartment to be on the thirty-fourth floor, and even if the character was capable of scaling that height, the sudden appearance of someone coming in a thirty-fourth floor window would scare the hell out of the characters and send the whole scene spinning off in the wrong direction. So yeah: it's a dumb note, but the executive is adamant about it and is this really a hill you want to die on?

If the answer to that question is *yes*, then take your time turning in the next draft. Extend it as far as you can without jeopardizing production schedules, then make sure to deliver the script to the executive in person, saying, "You know that note you gave about how I should have the character come in the door instead of the window, because it didn't make sense? I wasn't sure about it but I tried it and you were absolutely right, it's much better now."

By this point, the executive will vaguely remember having said something about a door and a window, but not much more than that, and upon hearing you admit that they were right, will shower you with benisons for your cooperative attitude without ever realizing that you just left it exactly the way it was.

Gentle reader, you have *no* idea how well that trick works.

Or how often I've used it.

Unfortunately that technique will never work for me again now that I've put it in this book. The things I do for you . . .

On every TV series I've ever produced, I have a standing policy that anyone in the cast or crew, down to the guy who sweeps the floor, can come up to me and say, "Joe, it sucks," and if they can explain why, and they're right, they get to stay. In some cases I've given bonuses to crew who have caught me in a massive dumbness, because it's better to correct that mistake at the script stage than have it air unaltered to a million viewers.

One final point on this subject.

When I wrote about not compromising the work, the image that came to mind was of some semi-hysterical dilettante in a beret (no, I don't know why a beret was in the picture, just work with me here) clutching his work to his chest and crying out, "No, no, no, *non*, you cannot touch my work, I am an ARTEEEST!"

Attitudes like that have nothing to do with professionalism and everything to do with ego, self-pride, and a truckload of insecurity.

Here's the corollary. Here's the point.

Let's say for the moment that you're a really good contractor. You know your stuff, you're a *professional*, which is why somebody just hired you to build them a house. So far, so good. Then one day, during construction, the guy who hired you points to a part of the house where, according to the blueprints, a load-bearing beam is about to be installed, and instructs you to put in something thinner and less resilient because it's cheaper.

You know the structure of this house like nobody else because you *designed* the freaking thing, so you know that if you put anything in that wall other than a proper load-bearing beam, sooner or later it will fail and the floor above will collapse, pancaking the house. Whether it happens this year, next year, or ten years after the original owner has sold it to someone else, sooner or later it *will* happen and it'll be your fault, and when the state housing commission asks why you put in the wrong kind of beam, "He told me to do it" won't get you out of trouble. So even though you risk being fired, you say no because you have to say no, and focus on what needs to be done to build a solid, secure house.

Resisting compromise should never be about ego, pride, or wanting it your way simply because that's the way you want it. It's not that you are an *arteest* in some terribly self-indulgent way, it's that you are a *professional* with an obligation to protect the structure you are building, even if that means arguing with the very person who hired you to build it. It is your duty to explain, clearly and precisely, why their suggestion works against the very thing they've asked you to create, in the hope of convincing them to go along with what's in the blueprints. If this fails, then you have to say no, and what happens next is what happens next.

When an audience reads a book or watches TV, they don't care that the actor was hungover during a crucial scene, that the director was having a bad day, or that the writer was forced to implement a note in chapter 9 that he or she knew from the start was moronic. They only care about the final result.

Your job, your *obligation*, is to make sure that the writing is solid, that the house doesn't collapse. That means being willing to listen to smart notes, and fight stupid notes.

Tell your story.

The rest will attend to itself.

AGENTS OF DARKNESS

As you continue to acquire credits, the small-fish-in-a-small-pond you have become will want to move into a bigger pond so you can continue your growth. In most cases this is going to require getting a literary agent or an agent specializing in film/TV. Since the latter is particularly difficult and comes with a whole host of issues specific to that industry, we'll address the former first.

Like most writers in Los Angeles, I've gone through a number of agents as my career grew or shifted and as the fortunes of the various agencies rose or fell. I was first repped by the Monteiro Rose Agency at a time when I (and the agency) worked almost exclusively in animation and lower-tier live action writers. I was with them for fifteen years, leaving only when I began working extensively as a show-runner, which was a bit beyond their expertise. Then in rapid succession I moved to the Gersh Agency, until we realized I was a bit more of a genre writer than Gersh was really known for; then went across the street to Broder Kurland Silbermann, leaving when it became clear that the relationship wasn't a good fit for either of us; landed at the United Talent Agency, until the agent at UTA indicated that he would only feel comfortable sending out my material if I wrote exactly what he told me to write exactly as he wanted me to write it, so I nuked the site from orbit (it's the only way to be sure) and moved to the Creative Artists Agency, where, after a less than stellar experience with an agent in the TV division, I lucked into Martin Spencer in 2006, who was then in CAA's film division but eventually came to represent me across all media.

I've been with Martin ever since, coming onto fifteen years. I stuck with him when he left CAA for Endeavor, then moved again later to Paradigm, where he was caught up in the agency's internal restructuring that booted out most of its TV/film agents. As I write this, Martin has made his next move, secure in the knowledge that where he goes, I go. Because as will be discussed in more detail later in this chapter, agent/client relationships are deeply personal, requiring absolute faith and trust from both parties. Hollywood may be a place of horror stories about agents, but when it works, when it's right, it makes all the difference. I stand where I am today primarily because of Martin's belief in me, confirming the importance of finding someone who will stand with you when nobody else will.

As writers begin their quest for an agent, they often complain, "You can't get a TV agent without credits, and you can't get credits without an agent—it's a Catch-22!" The statement seems true on its face, but is misleading when you dig a little deeper, so let's address those two clauses separately.

You can't get credits without an agent. This is true if you're talking about making a sale to major networks and studios, but there are plenty of small studios and independent producers who are always on the hunt for new material. It might be a low-budget film, a video project for a university, a fledgling production company, or a local director who wants to make a short film for distribution via various festivals, but there's always *someone* looking for a good script who can't afford Writers Guild rates and is precluded from going to an agented writer.

They're small credits but that's okay; you start modest, make a ton of mistakes, learn your craft, make some money, and work your way up until you can attract an agent's attention.

You can't get an agent without credits. This is somewhat but not entirely true, because if it *were* true then the roster of film and TV writers represented by the Writers Guild of America would have flatlined long ago. But every year, new writers sign their first contracts with agents and make their first significant sales. The numbers don't lie: The Writers Guild of America adds roughly 300 members per year to its roster, each of them a writer that has just made his or her first agented sale to a network or studio.

The real problem is that everybody's asking the wrong question. No one asks, *How do I catch a fish?* because the answer is obvious: You go fishing. The correct question is, *What is the best bait or lure to use to catch fish? What sort of food is the fish looking for?*

In this case, the question isn't *How do I get an agent?* It's *What is an agent looking for, and what's the best bait or lure to use to catch one?*

Finding the right agent is a courtship, and like any other kind of relationship, the other person wants to know that you're serious, that it's okay for them to invest years of time and energy into you because they *believe* in you, and that you're both working toward similar goals.

Okay, I get all that, but why is it so much harder to get a film/TV agent than any other kind of representative? It's all anyone ever talks about. Why do they have to make things so difficult?

Honestly, they're not. But the only way to understand that is to step back for a moment to see what you're really up against.

Old saying: *There's no shortage of love in the world, only of worthy vessels in which to put it.* If you want an agent, you have to prove that you're a worthy vessel, because there are a stunning number of flips, fakes, flakes, freaks, users, bozos, yo-yos, and yip-yops competing for their attention. That may sound like overstatement. It's not.

Every year, thousands of aspiring writers, actors, and self-described filmmakers come to Los Angeles, lured by the prospect of working in television or movies. What happens on the acting side is that the most attractive guys and gals in their hometown are told by friends and family, *You should go to Los Angeles and become a movie star!* Given the showbiz mythology that instant stardom requires only being in the right place at the right time, and that place is Los Angeles, they decide to hit the road. Many don't even bother to learn their craft because until now most things have come easy for them, and besides, they're more interested in being stars than actors.

When they arrive, they discover to their chagrin that the most attractive guys and gals from every *other* town in America (and Canada) have *also* shown up. Suddenly, they're no longer special, no longer *that one guy* or *that one gal*. To pay rent, they find work as food servers, baristas, or bartenders, the kind of jobs that leave plenty of time for making contacts, printing headshots, and doing the social circuit because as everybody *knows*, talent has nothing to do with becoming a star; it's all about who you *know*, except that's not actually true, and as weeks turn into months they slam into one wall after another.

By the six-month mark, about a third of them give up and go home. Of those that remain, some begin cramming acting lessons and workshops to make up for their lack of training, but it's often too little too late. The remainder, rather than put even that much effort into learning their craft, print more photos, take more headshots, create social media profiles, Instagram every waking moment of their lives, declare themselves brand ambassadors or social influencers, and spend night after night at clubs and parties in the futile hope of meeting casting directors or agents who will instantly recognize their talent. Slammed from false hope to false hope, they are preyed upon sexually, emotionally, and financially by those who have made a science of predatory behavior.

The only way to make the transition into a new stage of life, in or out of the entertainment industry, is to wrap yourself in a suit of armor made up of as much money as you can collect, then run through the fire as fast as you can in the desperate hope that your armor won't burn off before you reach the other side. Most of those coming to Los Angeles work out the usual equations of rent, supplies, food, and transportation, but fail to anticipate those who are just waiting for them to walk off the train or the plane so they can tear off as much of their armor as possible for themselves.

Every day their limited resources are sanded further down by paying for vanity "showcases" that almost never lead to jobs, managers who promise to find them work but want their fees paid in advance regardless of result, and investments in film and video projects that promise to feature their work but never materialize. As panic sets in, they take a second part-time job, and a third, and now the time spent earning the money needed to survive in Los Angeles doesn't leave time for them to pursue the very thing they came here to achieve in the first place. Despite working three jobs, they fall further behind, and now even their emergency savings are running out; the calendar is not their friend, and every lost day puts them that much closer to failure. They don't know where to turn, who to trust, what will work, or how to save themselves, and they're desperately afraid. Every day. *Afraid.*

Hollywood is a magnificent place where artists of every stripe can achieve their dreams, receiving all the fame, money, and recognition their talents deserve.

Hollywood is a place of unimaginable cruelty and virulent madness that will tear away everything you are and everything you could ever become, leaving behind nothing but an empty husk.

And before you come here, you must accept that *both* those descriptions are equally true, or it will destroy you.

(During the last phases of editing this manuscript, the editor on this book, Robb Pearlman, appended a note to the preceding paragraph reading, "So how exactly did you, self-described Awkward Person, make it through this madness?" The short version is: *barely*. The long version is detailed at length in my autobiography, *Becoming Superman*. Without belaboring the point or restating information available elsewhere, I will say only that—like everyone else in this town—there were times when I came within inches of losing it all, and survived only through the kindness of those who believed in me.)

The universally acknowledged truth of Los Angeles is that most of the folks who come here in search of success bounce off pretty fast; it's only after you've been in Los Angeles for three years that the town starts to take you seriously. So, by year two, most of the actors who came here in search of quick fame have given up, shattered and embittered by the experience. Most of them go home, usually in the spring after pilot season, when actors for new TV series have all been hired, but two groups stick around: the truly dedicated craftspeople who would rather die than give up on their art, and those whose egos cannot admit defeat, and look for alternate paths. *If I can't get hired as an actor, then I'll find another way in! I'll become a writer! And once I start writing movies and TV shows, I can create vehicles that I can star in!*

They come to this conclusion because everybody who can type thinks they can write. How hard could it be, really? It's just words, right? So now there are hundreds of untrained-actors-turned-untrained-*writers* competing with hundreds more newly-arrived writers and filmmakers, only a small percentage of whom have actual talent, training, and experience. Given all of *that*, it becomes clear that the agent isn't the problem—it's all the untalented whackjobs out there making life difficult for everyone else.

As bad as all that is, here's the horror, the truly awful part: Salted in among the pretenders and the poseurs, the fakes and the failures, are a small percentage of actors, writers, and filmmakers who have dedicated their lives to their craft, who have studied and fought and perfected their art to insane levels. Young people who could blow the doors off the entertainment industry. But you can't tell the real actors from the frauds until they are asked to audition, and that opportunity comes only rarely; can't tell the writers from the drones unless you read their material, and that chance is hard-won; can't tell the talented filmmakers from the rest unless you give them money to shoot something, and that goal is hardest of all. And talent does not confer wisdom or invulnerability; even the most gifted of those who come to Los Angeles often find themselves unprepared for the sometimes cruel reality that awaits them, and are preyed upon as readily as the others.

Finally, insert into our equation the hundreds of graduates who emerge each year from the film schools at UCLA, USC, AFI, NY Film Academy, and LA Film School, lean and hungry and ready to take on the world, and you have some idea of the crowd descending upon the offices of every agent in town.

Which brings us at last to this image: the waiting room at a boutique agency. After months or years of effort, ten people drawn from the pool described above have made it past the minefields, and are waiting to meet their prospective agents. For some of them it's their first shot at representation; for others it may be their *only* chance to find someone who can help guide them in their careers, someone who will care about them and help them and listen to them and return their calls,[1] the one person in all the world who can finally put them on the path to becoming television or film writers.

On the other side of the door, looking in through the frosted glass, is the agent, who despite introductory overtures has no *real* idea what's waiting out there when they call that person's name. It could be someone who talks a good game but lacks actual talent; a sociopath; a failed actor

---

1 Q: What do you get when you cross the Creative Artists Agency with a ham sandwich?
A: A ham sandwich that never returns your freaking phone calls.

pretending to be a writer; or maybe, just *maybe*, someone whose ability will merit months or years of deep personal investment. And bear in mind that the agent's credibility within the company is also on the line; choosing unwisely doesn't just waste the company's resources, it calls the agent's judgment into question.

Now do you understand why the wall is so high?

From the agent's perspective, the process of distinguishing fair from foul begins with evidence of raw talent and your willingness to put in the work needed to prove that you're serious and in this for the long haul. It's a hard and arduous process, but given everything described above, that's exactly as it should be.

Credits. As noted earlier, it's possible to acquire small credits by writing short films and getting them produced, but you can also demonstrate your talent by publishing articles or short stories in print or online. Agents are gatekeepers, so they will often look to other gatekeepers (editors and publishers) to help them home in on talent. Having someone who likes your work well enough to publish it, even in a small venue, is a measure of validation that can mean a lot to an agent. Even better if you've published fiction, because the "added value" of creating intellectual property that can be optioned by studios makes you more of an asset in the eyes of the agent.

Volume. The most common time-waster in Hollywood is the guy who writes one script (usually a pilot, which is utterly useless for reasons discussed elsewhere in this book) and stops there, expecting it to immediately attract an agent who will be overwhelmed by the wonderful ideas contained within. The problem with this scenario is that it never happens. There's a difference between wanting a career as a writer and wanting the pointy-hat that says *Once upon a time, I sold a script.* It's not about selling *a* script; it's about demonstrating the potential to sell dozens or hundreds of scripts as part of a career spanning decades. *That's* what an agent hopes for; *that's* what they're looking for.

Your first script is just that: your first script. You write that one, learn the lessons it holds for you, then write another, and another, and more after that until you get good at it. Going in with a script that says *I've never done this before* guarantees that you'll be booted out the door and never have another chance to rectify the damage. Ideally, you should go in with one or two feature film scripts and two or three scripts for TV series currently in production. This shows the agent that you can write established characters as well as your own creations, which is vital if you want to work on a series created by someone else (which is how most writers break into television).

The samples should demonstrate a healthy range of genres: a thriller, a character drama, light comedy, or other genres. Showcasing your professionalism, productivity, work ethic, and a wide breadth of material gives an agent the ammunition needed to sell your work and to sell *you*. A good TV writer is like a utility infielder, and a wide range of work gives the agent confidence that they can put you anywhere and you'll find a way to make it work.

Once you have enough samples, you can start contacting agents. Your first stop is the Writers Guild of America website (www.wga.org), which provides a list of signatory agencies and, in many cases, whether or not they're open to new clients. (A signatory agency is one that has accepted the WGA's fundamental rules governing how clients are treated, what fees can be commissioned, and so forth. This is preferable to going to a non-signatory agency where there are no such safeguards.) You're not likely to get traction with such major agencies as Creative Artists, United Talent, or William Morris/Endeavor so start small. Boutique agencies are more open to new voices because as their clients become more successful, they will often move on to larger agencies capable of addressing their expanded needs, which creates opportunities for new clients.

Once you've got your list of agencies, reach out to five to ten at a time with a professional, courteous letter or email explaining who you are, what your goals are, why you think you're a good fit for their agency, and, without going into too much detail, what scripts you have available as samples of your work. Do *not* send the scripts in cold, because the agency will refuse to look at them for legal reasons. Most of them will simply roundfile the letters and forget them, and that's okay. It's a numbers game, like asking someone out on a date; you're going to be turned down a lot before you find someone who finds you intriguing.

Once your work has attracted the attention of an agent, they will usually invite you to lunch, coffee, or an office meeting to scope you out. It's important to remember during these meetings that it's not just about the quality of the work. This is the courtship round, where the agent decides if you're someone he or she would enjoy working with for months or years to come. Don't be defensive, don't talk about how hard the town is (the agent already knows this), don't be jaded, bitter, or abrasive; in short, don't be a jerk. Agents are very cognizant of the PITA (Pain in the Ass) Rule, and if that's how you come across, the agent will decline to represent your work. Instead, talk about your dreams and goals, what sort of shows you would love to work for, and where you see yourself five years down the road. Be clever, charming, entertaining, and *local*, or at least willing to give that impression. If you want to break into TV or movies, you *must* live in Los Angeles. This shows that you're committed enough to your career to make the geographic leap of faith. If you can't afford to make that move, tell the agent that you're in the process of doing so, or use a friend's address as your own and fake it for a while.

What happens next depends on your mutual chemistry and the quality of your work. If you get turned down, move on to the next agency and try again. If the talent is there, sooner or later somebody will want to represent you.

Getting a literary agent, one that specializes in prose, is a bit more straightforward because there aren't as many starstruck neophyte writers trying to break down their doors. Writers don't get into novels because they think they're going to become millionaires overnight; they know that they'll probably have to keep their day jobs to survive, but that doesn't matter—they're in it for the stories they want to tell.

The more credibility you can bring to the table when approaching an agent, the better you will be received, so again, having a list of articles, reviews, or short stories in print shows that you're serious, but you're still going to have to write a novel end to end for submission purposes. This helps address any questions an agent may have about your talent, and weeds out the fakes: Lots of people *start* writing novels but only a small percentage *finish* them, and fewer still produce material of even amateur quality. If you have the time and wherewithal to write a second novel as your submission, that would be even better because that book would incorporate all the lessons you learned while writing the first one. But not everyone can afford the time involved with that step, so it's vital to make the manuscript as good as you can.

It's common for new writers to hit the end of a novel and think, *Okay, I'm done, it's perfect the way it is.* We believe this partly out of ego, and largely out of a reluctance to heavily revise a five- or six-hundred-page manuscript. But editing is where a *manuscript* turns into a *novel*, allowing you to fine-tune the writing, the dialogue, and the characters. Agents want to see polished, professional manuscripts, not a flawed first draft, and if you *don't* make these revisions, within minutes of sending out the submission draft you'll open the file to check on something and *the very first thing you will see* is a typo or a poorly written phrase. *Always.* I don't know *why* it happens, I only know *that* it happens and that this level of random cruelty almost certainly demonstrates the absence of a just and merciful god.

The submission process is much the same as with TV/film agents: you can choose a likely prospect from published lists of agencies open to new clients, or pick up books by writers who work in the same genre as yourself, check the indicia page that (usually) lists their agents, and search online to find them. You then fire off introductory letters or emails similar to what was described in the preceding section and hope for the best.

The good news is that in these days of vertical integration, many literary agencies have ongoing relationships or partnerships with TV/film agencies, and vice versa, so when you get one, you can potentially inherit the other.

Finding an agent willing to take on a fledgling writer is difficult; finding the *right* agent is *ridiculously* difficult. But it happens. Every day. Because just as writers need agents, agents need writers. They just need to know that you're serious, that you're committed, and that you have talent.

Easy-peasy, right?

IMPOSTER SYNDROME

For just a moment, let's pretend that only one copy of this book has ever been sold.[1] No one else is privy to this conversation. We can talk privately, just you and me.

So let's talk about your problem.

Not that one, the *other* one . . . I'm a writer, not a sorcerer.

You've been doing this for a while, you have acquired a fair number of published or produced credits, and you've actually been able to make a living of one sort or another off your writing. But despite the sales, the reviews, the accolades, and your family telling you they're proud of you (for a change) . . . you still feel like an imposter.

Here's a secret: We *all* feel that way. Every day I await a knock at the door, where a man waiting outside will explain that my writing career was actually intended for someone else but got delivered here by mistake, and the proper owner wants it back.

Imposter syndrome usually has its roots in two internal monologues.

1. I don't write the stories—they come from somewhere outside—so if it's not me, how can I ever really take credit for any of it?

On one level, you're not wrong. As noted in the chapter about awaiting the Muse, no one *really* knows where stories come from. We can sometimes point to an inspiration that *started* the process, or some dialogue between

---

1 The *thud!* you just heard was my publisher having a myocardial infarction.

the characters that came out of a prior relationship, but there's a long road between that flash of thought and an actual *story*.

Stories accrete like lint on a sweater; you observe little things that get lodged in the filter of your subconscious, you start making connections between this idea over *here* and that factoid way the hell over *there* . . . and one day you brush your hand down the front of your sweater and *ta-daaaa*, there's a story. The process is mysterious and elusive and frustrating. But it's still *you* at the center of it all, still your experiences that shape the process. Even if we accept for a moment that stories *do* come from somewhere else, that some aspect of the zeitgeist or the universal gestalt seizes a moment out of history to tell us *this* story at *this* moment . . . if it is true that we are only the receiver, not the signal, then whatever chose to speak to the world through us did so because we alone were on the right frequency at the right time.

On April 15, 1912, twenty-one-year-old telegraphist Harold Cottam was in the right place and the right time to pick up the distress signal from the *Titanic*. His actions in swiftly relaying that information to the *Carpathia* saved hundreds of lives. Nobody after the fact said, *Big deal, the signal came from somewhere else, you didn't invent it.* He got the signal, he acted on it, and saved lives. There's no shame and much regard in being chosen by the universe to bring something new into the world, a story capable of touching people who find themselves in circumstances similar to those endured by your characters and are looking for something to give them hope so they can keep going.

Put more simply: Maybe you're right about the story coming from somewhere *out there*, and maybe you ain't, but since we'll never know the truth one way or the other, you may as well embrace the nightmare, accept the applause, and move on.

2. What's the point of being a writer if everything has already been said? I'm just rehashing what other writers smarter and more talented than me wrote a hundred years ago.

Once again, you're not wrong. Themes of war, love, loss, death, success, tragedy, existence, exploration, revelation, and exaltation have been done in every form of literature and storytelling going back to the first proto-human who placed his hand against a cave wall and blew ink from plants onto it, creating a five-fingered silhouette that proclaimed to the world *I exist, I am here*.

As André Gide wrote, "Everything has been said before, but since nobody listens we have to keep going back and beginning all over again." Writers in the eighteenth and nineteenth centuries had some very wise things to say about life and death and meaning . . . but they told those truths, or more accurately their *versions* of those truths, before cell phones and radio and penicillin and radium and Buddy Holly and Gandhi. Truth is informed by context and filtered through the writer's unique perspective, and with each new generation those truths must be reexamined, reconsidered, and reinvented. No one has seen the world as you do, because you live in a world very different than the one that existed one hundred years ago.

In 1906, Upton Sinclair wrote an exposé of the meatpacking industry entitled *The Jungle* that shocked the nation and led to the creation of new laws that made the industry slightly less horrific. But *The Jungle* does not address twenty-first-century sweatshops or the tragedy of child labor. The social aspects of prostitution were examined in Shakespeare's *Measure for Measure*, as well as in the works of Charles Dickens, Maupassant, and Colette, but there are no words in any of them that touch upon the problem of today's international sex-slave trade.

Your perspective is your own, and what you say has never been said before in the way in which you will say it.

There's one other reason why most writers feel like fakes, frauds, and imposters, and it may be the most important of them all.

It's about being a magician.

Like writers, most magicians start honing their craft at an early age, learning the techniques and tricks of others, then slowly adapting those methods to fit their own voices. The problem is that when they begin to perform, and the audience applauds the moment of magic they have just witnessed, the magician cannot entirely accept the praise for doing something impossible because unlike the audience *he knows how the trick was done*. He knew that by placing the mirror just *here*, and the secret door behind the curtain over *there*, that when the flash happened at stage right the audience wouldn't see the assistant going from point A to point B on stage left in a magnificent display of astral projection.

But it *wasn't* astral projection, just something that sorta-kinda looked like it.

Everything a magician does is fake. Literally, a trick.

And every magician knows this.

Which may explain why I've encountered so few magicians who seem genuinely happy, even when the applause rocks the house.

(Several years ago, I had occasion to work with Penn Gillette, 50 percent of the famous team of Penn & Teller. As I watched him over the course of several days, he was constantly on the phone, yelling angrily about one thing or another. The cast and crew did all they could to cheer him up, but he would not be cheered. I was frantically busy with production and didn't have a chance to spend any time with Penn until his last day of work, when I found myself sitting at a lunch table across from him. I was a big fan of his work but I've always been a bit shy so I was looking for a way into a conversation when I noticed something.

("So," I asked, "why is one of your fingernails painted red?"

(His reply: "To remind me that I once killed a man for asking personal questions." Then he stalked off to make another angry phone call.)

Writers make up stories in their heads about things that never happened but which feel as if they did. Using a collection of techniques and stylistic tricks, we fool the reader or the audience into accepting the reality of the emotions the characters are expressing. But none of it's actually *real*, so when the applause comes, there is a part of us that can't quite accept the accolades because, like the magician, we know how the trick was done.

So what can we do here, together, right now, to help you deal with your feelings of being an imposter?

There is only this.

A guy goes to see a fortune-teller. She glances at his palm then shakes her head. "For the next ten years," she says, "you're going to lose every job you hold, you will lose love, and there will be sickness, and poverty, and every day for those ten years you are going to feel absolutely *awful* about it."

"What happens after the ten years?" he asks.

She shrugs. "You'll get used to it."

Imposter syndrome is part of the price we pay for what we do. It's the useful fear that keeps us constantly striving to improve our work, and it will never entirely go away.

But you'll get used to it.

ANNNND HERE'S THE PITCH

All writers start their careers from the same paradigm: you write something, you send it out, and with luck, you sell it. So you write the next thing. Send it out. Probably have a slightly better chance of selling it based on the prior sale. Write. Send. Sell. Rinse. Repeat. After you've been doing this for a while, editors and executives come to trust your work and open the door to giving you assignments. The glory of this upgrade is that you're not flying blind, you have a home for your work, *and* you can get paid while writing rather than waiting until after the work is done. The downside is that they're going to want at least *some* idea of what your story is about before cutting a check or a contract, so you need to be able to pitch the story verbally in a way that catches their interest.

Pitching receives the most attention in the worlds of TV and film, but every aspect of the writing profession requires pitching in one form or another. If you've sold a novel written on spec, and you're hoping for a contract on book number two, your agent or editor is going to ask, "So, what do you want to write next? What's the book about?" When that happens, it behooves you to be able to answer in more than vague generalities.

Journalism is no different. Whenever I've had an ongoing relationship with a newspaper or magazine, every assignment began with me calling or meeting with the editor to tell him or her what story I wanted to cover next.

And. I. *Hated*. It. Always have, always will. There are no words to convey the degree to which I abhor the pitching process. If I wanted to be a performer or a trained monkey, I would've majored in Drama or gone into politics. I'm far more comfortable alone behind a keyboard than I am trying to entertain a room full of strangers with money on the line. Pitching favors glad-handers, glib speakers, and superficiality, even when the actual writing talent isn't there, and often penalizes those who are by nature shy, reclusive, socially maladroit, or, more simply, *writers*.

But it's an inescapable part of the business, and we have to learn how to do it well if we want to take our careers to the next level. So here are some pointers to get past the worst of the learning curve, based both on my own experience pitching and years spent on the other side of the desk as a producer, listening to writers pitch their hearts out, seeing what they did right to get an assignment, and where they ultimately sabotaged themselves through fear or inexperience.

1) THE TWENTY-MINUTE RULE

I'm putting this ahead of the creative considerations because in many ways it's the most important. Once you're in the room and start pitching to an editor or an executive, it's rare for them to cut you off at the midpoint because it's considered rude, a breach of protocol. For all intents and purposes, you own them for that window of time, so it's in your vested interest not to commit the crime of death by pitching.

Assuming an hour-long meeting, the rule of thumb is five to ten minutes amiable chatter, twenty minutes to pitch, ten to fifteen minutes to discuss the pitch, then you're out the door, giving the executive ten minutes or so to catch their breath, check messages, and collect their thoughts in preparation for the next meeting. It's rational, polite, and respectful. Despite this, I have had writers come into my office to pitch stories where it took them an hour *or more* to go from "Here's what I've come up with" to "What do you think?" And because every detail was excruciatingly rendered, the writer often had to stop and check their notes, creating awkward pauses before droning on again. Worst of all, by now I can usually see where the story is going but I can't interrupt without being rude, so I'm stuck, and by the time we sail past the one-hour mark, any chance the writer might have had to make the sale is lost to blind, unremitting rage.

Twenty minutes. Seriously. Please.

2) EXCITEMENT MATTERS

When you step into the office of an editor, publisher, or producer, remember that they have publication schedules or broadcast schedules to meet, so each assignment they can lock down is one less hole they need to fill. They *want* you to succeed, and the chief metric determining success is the degree to which you can get them excited about your story, because most of the pitches they suffer through fail to accomplish that. Yes, the writer explains how A goes to B goes to C, but *telling* someone a story isn't the same thing as *engaging* the other person emotionally in what you're pitching. The first is exposition; the latter is a pitch.

One of the ways to achieve this is to pull them in on a personal level, talking *with* them instead of *at* them in a prolonged twenty-minute monologue. If you're pitching a story about the difficulties between parents and their children, it's okay to say to the executive, "When you were growing up, did this kind of thing happen to you, and what did you think of it?" Inviting them to engage with you in the storytelling makes it feel more like a conversation, and turns them into something other than a passive target for your words.

It also helps to know the background of the person to whom you're pitching. If they previously published or produced a work in a similar category to what you're describing, it's okay to allude to it. "I understand you worked on *Harrison's Highway*, which I really loved,[1] so you know what it's like when a main character just takes off one day to see the world." Suddenly the executive not only feels *seen*, they can integrate what you're describing with something they did before that may have great personal significance. It also shows that you took the time to find out more about the executive, and whenever someone makes an effort to show interest in us, we immediately like them better.

If the idea of pitching still gives you a case of the screaming willies, it may be wise to spend some time rehearsing in front of a camera. Playing back the video may be painful, but it will tell you where you need to sit up, breathe, or amp up the volume. Keep rehearsing until it feels unrehearsed,

---

1 Even if you didn't. *Especially* if you didn't.

adding little asides that can seem spontaneous in the room. If you can be the most exciting thing they've seen that day, it vastly increases your odds of getting the assignment.

3) WHY IT MATTERS TO YOU

This point is best illustrated through example.

During my tenure on *The Twilight Zone*, we took pitches from as many as five writers per day, three or four days per week. Most of these were stories we'd heard a hundred times before ("And at the end we discover they're robots!" or "And at the end we discover they're all actually dead!"), or which had been written infinitely better in the original *TZ* series. If there was something that clicked, I'd ask why the story mattered to them. Very few had good answers, focused primarily on why it felt like *The Twilight Zone* to them, and how much they liked the gimmick or the twist ending. Not having a good answer to that question didn't preclude us from buying a pitch if it was something that set the room on fire, but it could sometimes make all the difference if we were on the fence.

Because whether you're an editor or a producer or a network or studio executive, you want your writers and your stories to *burn*.

One day, a writer named William Selby walked into our offices for a pitch session based on a sample script, submitted by his agent, which was quite good. But at this stage of his career he hadn't actually sold anything to television, not a single produced credit, so there was some concern in the room about whether or not he had the chops to write for *The Twilight Zone*, which was considered a plum assignment around town. Competition for assignments was stiff, so new writers had a *lot* to prove.

He'd come armed with three stories. The first didn't catch our attention and felt a bit by-the-numbers, so we passed. The second story paralleled something we were already developing, so that one also fell by the wayside. His third and final pitch, "The Hellgrammite Method," was about an alcoholic desperate to kick the habit. His search leads him to a doctor who offers a cure that works by taking just one pill. What our protagonist doesn't know is that the pill contains a variation on the

Hellgrammite worm that will kill him if he ingests any more alcohol, ever.

As he spun out the story, I saw a light come into his eyes that had been absent during the first two pitches. So when he reached the end, I asked the same question I'd asked of so many others: "Why does this story matter to you?"

I could see he was uncomfortable with the question, so he started talking about how timely the story was, the social significance of the subject matter, the way it worked within the classic *Twilight Zone* structure—

I cut him off, something I almost never do. "I didn't ask why it might matter to someone *else*, I asked why it matters to *you*."

It took a while, but eventually we drilled down to the truth I'd sensed in his pitch: He came from a family where there had been issues with alcoholism, and writing this story would let him address a past that clearly still tormented him.

After he left the room, executive producer Mark Shelmerdine started back toward his office, not having heard anything that jumped out at him, when I said, "I think we should buy 'Hellgrammite.'"

He turned, surprised to hear my reaction. "Why?"

"Because he burns to tell this story," I said. "It was right there in his eyes. He *needs* to write this out of his system, and the truth behind the story will give it a sense of authenticity that will make the fantastical parts feel more real."

"He doesn't have any credits," Mark said.

"I know. But we should buy it anyway, because he knows that he has something to prove, and that will give him one more reason to work his ass off and write the best script possible."

Mark hesitated, still unsure, but he respected my opinion, and I could see he was starting to waffle.

"I'll make a deal with you," I said. "I'll backstop him. If the script comes in and it's awful, I'll do the rewrite and get it up to snuff."

"Okay," he said reluctantly, "but this is one of the last assignments we have open—we're almost out of money for script development, so if it doesn't work out, it's on you."

"Fair deal," I said.

When William's script arrived several weeks later, it was *solid*. The script burned because *he* burned, and it required very little work on my part. We not only produced it with Timothy Bottoms cast as our protagonist, the episode went on to win the prestigious Scott Newman Award, founded by Scott's father, actor Paul Newman, for its frank portrayal of alcoholism.

We bought that story because passion is hard to find in the day-to-day grind of television; because it *mattered* to him.

So if the story you pitch matters to you, take the time to explain *why* it's important that you tell this story, and that there's no one else who can tell it as well as you because nobody else has the perspective or the personal experience to tell it well. It makes a difference.

And if the story *isn't* important to you, if it *doesn't* matter, then you shouldn't be pitching the damned thing in the first place.

4) DO THE WORK

Just as pitches shouldn't be too long, coming in too short is also problematic because it shows that you didn't take the time to think the story through. The most extreme example of this came while I was working as a producer on a mystery series and a writer came in to pitch for an assignment. We sat across from each other in my office. Chatted. At the ten-minute mark I could see him straighten, ready to go. Spot on.

"Okay," I said, "so what story have you got for me?"

He leaned in, very excited, and said, "Amnesia."

He stopped there. Settled back on the couch. Very proud of himself.

It took me a moment to respond. "Sorry?"

"Amnesia!" he fired back, even more proud of himself.

"So . . . amnesia, albatross, things that begin with the letter A? What are we talking about here?"

"Well, I was just thinking that amnesia stories are always popular, and we could work out the details between us."

"So that's all you've got?"

"Yes."

So no, he didn't walk out the door with an assignment.

Frankly, he's lucky he made it out the door at all.

Here is how most successful pitches are structured:

Begin with a brief introduction to the story and why you want to tell it.

Give us the characters: who they are and how they relate to one another.

Then give us the story: how we get into it, the major beats needed to understand where the story is going, and how we get out of it. If it's for TV, break it down by acts because, unlike film, there are often commercial breaks to be considered. If it's for prose, go straight through, highlighting the essential moments without getting lost in the details. Keep it moving.

Characters come first in the pitch rather than the story because we can visualize characters and remember them more readily than plot twists that can feel disconnected in the abstract. This gives the executive a baseline of interesting people upon whom you can begin piling the details. After all, stories told at parties tend to begin with, "Did you hear what happened to Bob?" rather than starting with a long explanation of what happens if you climb over the top of the lion's cage before finally mentioning twenty minutes in that this happened to Bob from Accounting. If you can get the listener to care about your characters before launching into the plot, you're halfway there.

One helpful hint that applies more to script pitches than prose (though I've had it come up a few times in the latter category) covers what to say when they ask, "How do you see the tone of it?" In the past, whenever an executive asked this, I assumed they were asking if the feel of the piece was light, dark, or irreverent, and answered accordingly. Each time I was mystified when none of those explanations seemed to satisfy them. It was years before my agent at the time clarified the situation.

"When they ask 'what's the tone,' they're not *actually* asking what the literal tone is. They're asking what it's *like*, what other movie or TV show is similar in feel and approach."

"But isn't the whole point of creating a series to make something new, something that's not like anything else out there?"

The agent waved off the question. "Nobody wants to take a chance on something nobody else is doing or has done. Scares the hell out of them. They want something successful to compare it against so they can visualize it. Remember also that if an exec approves a project and it tanks, it could cost him his job. Being able to point to something similar that succeeded can help justify their decision to pick up your pitch in case it doesn't work out. But by the same token, they don't want the comparison to be so over-exposed that everyone's doing it. They want to jump on the bandwagon, not be run over by it.

"In this town," he said, "everybody wants to be first to be second."

5) THE CHEAT SHEET

One of the reasons people freeze up during pitches is that they're too close to the story to be objective in describing it to a third party. They're wedded to going through every beat, no matter how obscure, unable to translate their ideas into a clear, concise, easily communicated pitch. So if none of the preceding methods solve this, here's a trick you can resort to when necessary.

Rather than putting your ego on the line, pretend that last night you went out with friends (which for most writers will start with pretending they have friends) to see a movie (which just happens to be the story you've been developing). The film was funny, poignant, and moving; full of action and suspense and great characters and, really, just the best movie you've seen in ages.

Now it's the next morning, and you've run into another imaginary friend at the coffee shop. As you await your cafe latte, you mention that you saw this really great movie the other day.

"What's it about?" your friend asks.

And you describe it in the same terms everyone else uses when asked that question: it was about *this*, it had a great character over here, another over there, and *then* . . . you hit the highlights because your friend doesn't want to hear every last detail, and besides, your order is about to land on the counter. But you want him to see the film, to have that shared experience, so you do your best to sell him on why it's worth his time.

That is how you pitch your story, as though it were something you saw up on the big screen the night before and are describing to a friend. It takes the onus off you as the creator, makes the process fun, and most of the time it works out really well in the room. It generally doesn't run as long or as detailed as a full pitch, probably averaging about ten to fifteen minutes, but it still shows that you did your homework.

This approach also works well with agents and interviews with members of the press about whatever project you're currently involved with.

Before wrapping up this chapter, I want to pass along one final hint about pitching to the nascent or working TV writers reading this, a little secret that I promise will change your lives.

I don't think that I'm going too far out on a limb to say that most actors working in supporting roles on TV series are human beings, and as such they have needs and desires and dreams. They also have agents who spend a great deal of time on the phone with the producers asking (sometimes quite loudly) for more screen-time, more lines, and more exposure for their clients. The more really cool scenes an actor has on a series, the more stories at which he/she is the center, the better the deal they can make on the next show that wants to hire them.

I'm not saying I've received those calls. I'm just saying that from time to time I've had an aneurysm while speaking on the phone.

When writers pitch on TV series they almost always walk in with stories about the lead character, in which the supporting cast are an afterthought at best. This is absolutely natural and understandable. But it does nothing to stop the phone calls.

So if you can walk in the door with a story that strongly features a supporting cast member, putting him or her at the center of the action without short-shrifting the lead, the producer will burst into tears of gratitude, buy the script, and adopt you as a long-lost child.

I've been that writer, and I've been that producer. Trust me, this works.

Verbally pitching stories to agents, editors, publishers, or producers is difficult for many writers because we don't really consider it a part of the work itself. The writing impulse starts between neurons, races down a tracery of nerves to the fingers, and out the other side. We type it more than we say it. If anything, we learn *not* to talk too much about our stories because it takes the lid off the pressure cooker, releasing the tension we need to push through the writing process. And in the beginning of a writer's career, it isn't generally necessary; the work does all the talking for us. It's only with some measure of success that pitching even becomes an option. But once we accept the necessity of pitching and learn how to do it reasonably well, we can start getting assignments that can help us achieve stability and consistency.

Meanwhile, it's absolutely okay to hate every part of that process.

That's why God made therapists.

SEVERAL HUNDRED WORDS ABOUT WRITER'S BLOCK

I don't believe in writer's block.

More to the point: Writer's block doesn't exist.

That doesn't mean that the process is seamless or that it doesn't dead-end from time to time. The trick is recognizing the problem for what it is rather fearing it for what it isn't. There's no cure for something as ambiguous as "writer's block" because there's no clearly defined cause, and thus no apparent remedy. For many writers that sense of helplessness and hopelessness can be terrifying. They can languish for months as they wait for the Demon Writer's Block to let go, surrendering their authority, agency, and control to the whims of an uncaring universe.

Piffle.

There are three primary causes of what is referred to as "writer's block," all of which are eminently within the writer's power to control and fix.

PLATEAUING

The upward arc of a writer is not a straight line but rather a series of steps. We work hard, achieve progress in our work, and keep going along that plateau until we hit the wall at the far end that signals we've learned all that can be learned at this stage. It's then up to us to scramble over the top to the next step, where the process of work and learning begins again. Plateaus are not only normal, they are essential to the creative process because they are designated points of growth, like pencil marks on the door measuring your height as you grow. Each plateau marks a point of transition between where you were yesterday, where you are now, and where you're about to land next. The danger comes when we see the wall and fail to realize that there's another step overhead that we can't see, but which can be reached with time, effort, and patience.

It's not "writer's block," it's recalibration.

Every time we finish a project we earn another tool for our toolbox. Those tools let us understand what we just created, reveal the flaws that were previously invisible to us, and let us begin writing the *next* thing in a slightly elevated position from where we were when we started the *last* thing. Tools are all about incremental improvements that aggregate over time until we reach a point where we recognize that what we're doing *now* is better than what we did *before* but not as good as what we *want* to be doing, or what we think we *should* be doing, at this stage. We have enough tools and experience to be dissatisfied with where we *are* but still lack clarity about how to get where we *want* to be. We can only trust that the growth process this time will resolve itself the same way it did when we acquired all the previous tools.

Plateaus also serve to remind you that in addition to creating art, you are creating yourself as an artist. The tools that let you understand what the earlier stories meant and what they were trying to say are also a part of the process that lets you understand what *you* mean and what *you* want to say as an artist. Just as those stories change over time, who you are and what you want to communicate through the work also grows and changes.

We start by deciding to make art, then gradually realize that it's the art that makes us. The writer you are after penning thirty scripts, stories, or books is not the same writer who began that process, and if you're not conscious of that change, if you're still using last week's solutions to solve this week's problem, a disconnect starts to grow between who you are and what you're creating. It may be as simple as your brain saying it's tired of writing the same kind of story all the time. Nobody wants to eat the same meal every day. But now you're caught between the security of writing something familiar that you can sell and the risk of trying something new and untried. The unresolved cognitive dissonance bounces between those two poles faster and faster until a circuit blows and suddenly you feel blocked, not because you don't know how to write but because you're at war with yourself, and with your art.

Again: you don't *make* art happen, you *let* art happen, and if the art ain't happening, it's not because it's gone away or deserted you, it's because you or some aspect of you is standing in the way.

The solution is to not panic or to try to force the process. The work has paused because the creative part of your brain is saying, *I need to think this through—can you just feed me for a while as I work this out?* Allow that space to happen. Read books. Watch movies. Listen to music. Feed the Muse. Don't just stare at the screen and fume. Trying to solve an equation while someone is yelling WHAT'S THE ANSWER? only makes it harder to find the solution.

You can also take this pause as an opportunity to think about what matters to you as a writer at this moment in your life: How do you feel about what you've written to this point, are there themes you've exhausted or new ideas you're passionate about, and what's driving you forward on a purely emotional basis? Give yourself room to acknowledge the writer you are now versus who you were previously, because the art is trying to tell you that those things may no longer be the same. An open dialogue between your heart and your talent will often provide the tools you need to get past the plateau and climb up to the next step.

Antoine de Saint-Exupéry's *The Little Prince* talks about the process of taming the fox. If you chase after it or set a trap for it, the fox will elude you. Sometimes the only way to tame the fox is to turn your back on it and look away, allowing it to approach you on its own terms. The more you chase the story, the more it will remain just beyond your reach; turn your back on it like you're not interested, and in many cases it will come to you.

ACKNOWLEDGING THE WRONG TURN

Another issue misperceived as "writer's block" arises when the logical part of the brain is trying to tell the artistic part of the brain *You screwed up six miles back down that road, pal*, but we refuse to listen.

No writer deep in the process of creating a major work wants to hear that they messed up during the early stages, because that means going back and rewriting a good chunk of what they just spent the last few days, weeks, or months creating. When one part of the brain refuses to acknowledge a mistake, and the other part refuses to go forward until the problem is fixed, we end up like a monkey with its hand around a nut in a jar: it can't pull it out and it won't let go.

This is why so many early novels or scripts go unfinished. Midway through the work, the writer has just enough tools to recognize that they made a huge misstep X pages ago, but they don't have the heart to go back and rewrite everything. So they put the project in a drawer and start something else, only to see *the same thing happen* because they never finished the prior project and thus never acquired the tools that would have shown them how to avoid making that mistake in future.

When we get stuck in Act Three of a play, or in the Complication stage of a novel, it's easy to think that this must be where the problem is. But a problem in Act Three is often a problem in Act Two, just as a problem in Act Two is usually a problem in Act One. We crashed into the tree over *here*, but the tree isn't the issue; the problem started when we drove off the road half a mile back *thataway*. We think the tree is writer's block. It's not. It's just a signpost saying *go back and try this again*.

Once we finally face the fact that we made a mistake ten, fifty, or a hundred pages back, and commit to fixing it and revising everything that followed, the block often goes away. We've cleared the debris and can go back to telling the story we wanted to tell in the first place, which is smarter than it would've been if we'd left those mistakes in place.

WE'RE NOT READY

Much of the writing process involves getting to know your characters well enough so that whatever situation you drop them into, all you have to do is sit back, watch what they do, and write it down. But for this to work, you *and* your characters have to know as much about themselves as possible. If you've only given superficial consideration to their pasts, their goals, their mistakes, families, passions, and pathologies, then you and they have little to work with in reacting to whatever scenario you've created. Over time this can make their choices feel flat and repetitive. When an artist gets bored with what they're creating, everything comes to a screeching halt because a part of you knows that if *you're* bored writing a particular character, you can only *imagine* how bored the audience will be while reading it.

And frankly, sometimes the creative part of your brain knows that you're not yet ready to write whatever you've decided you want to tackle next, and keeps throwing out the anchor to slow down the process. I had a rough story worked out for the movie *Changeling* years before I finally got a draft I liked, because I didn't have the tools, the information, or the techniques needed to wrestle that beast to the ground. So the creative part of my brain dug in its heels and refused to let me move forward. *Come back when you're older and smarter, kid.*

One way out of this is to dig deeper into your characters by using what screenwriters call "mood boards." Get a bulletin board and start pinning up photos, newspaper articles, statistics, slang, anything that can inform your characters' background and interests.

We used the mood boards during the Netflix series *Sense8* to help us develop our characters. Eventually the boards got too cluttered, but the moment the boards hit maximum capacity was *also* the moment when the characters finally became fully realized, sufficiently "alive" to make their own decisions and react authentically to whatever situations presented themselves.

During his work as an editor at the *Territorial Enterprise*, Mark Twain had a desk built to his specifications that was topped by a cabinet whose front was marked with thirty square holes. He would start a story, and if he discovered that it didn't want to get written yet, or that he didn't yet have the tools needed to finish it, he'd stuff the pages into one of the holes and move on to the next filed story. He'd start at the top of the cabinet, pulling out pages and asking in each case, *Can I finish this now?* and if the answer came back *Yes*, he'd pick up where he left off and keep going. If not, or if it stalled out after a while, the pages went back into the hole and he moved on to the next one. Sometimes you just have to put the work up on the shelf and let it straighten itself out for a while rather than trying to force the issue.

The more you know about yourself, why you're doing what you're doing, the kind of art you want to make, the kind of art you *don't* want to make, who you are and who you're writing about, the smaller the odds of the work grinding to a halt, and the easier it is to dig yourself out if it does happen.

There is no such thing as writer's block, any more than there is such a thing as a nervous breakdown. The nerves don't break down. There's not a CAT scan in existence that can find a broken nerve in a nervous breakdown or a physical block that suddenly appeared in your cerebral cortex. In both cases, the problem starts when you receive more emotional or mental input than you can handle, so you shut down. There's too little clarity and too much static in the broadcast, so you switch it off. There's nothing actually preventing the creation of stories, no interruptions in neural service, nothing physical between you and the act of writing. You've just lost your way and need to figure out a way back.

Frustration achieves nothing. So, while navigating the neural landscape, remember to be gentle with yourself. Sooner or later, you'll find your way back to the light.

TURNING IT UPSIDE DOWN

While working on *The Twilight Zone*, I wrote a script entitled "Dream Me a Life" about the resident of a retirement home who shut himself off long ago from friends and family. Then, one day, he begins sharing the nightmares of a catatonic woman in a room across the hall and is pulled into a terrifying situation where he must intervene to save her life. I liked the symmetry of the storytelling: a man who has chosen emotional isolation has to rescue a woman who is also incapable of reaching out to others, but for very different reasons. In her recurring dream she's in a room where something is trying to break through a locked door; she begs our main character for help, saying that if it comes through she will die. But he wants nothing to do with her dreams or her problems, especially when he discovers that a wound incurred in her dream translates to a real injury when he wakes up.

The two threads come together as we learn that his solitude is the result of rage and guilt over his inability to help his wife as she was dying during a prolonged sickness. The realization that he has the chance to do for this woman what he couldn't do for his wife gives him the courage to destroy the darkness on the other side of the door, a creature that has been feeding on her guilt over her husband's death. This gives them both closure, and as she emerges from her coma, he comes out of his shell.

After finishing the draft, I gave it to my then-wife and asked her to give it a read.

When she turned the last page, she nodded for a minute, then said, "Yeah, it's okay."

If there are any two words every artist fears when their work is assessed, *It's okay* is right at the top of the list. It means the story has earned neither praise nor alarm, it's not super-good or super-bad, not cold or hot . . . just *okay*. I'd rather write something dreadful while striving for better than face the awfulness of *It's okay*.

"You're always saying that a story should never end on its premise, but that's kind of what this does," she explained. "You set up that something terrible behind the door is going to kill her unless he saves her. He stops the terrible thing behind the door and saves her. And that's fine, there are some great scenes in here. I guess I was just hoping for more than that."

I took back the script, stalked back to my office, and closed the door, thinking, *I'm an artist and this is a great script—what the hell does* she *know?*

Except, of course, she was right, and I knew she was right. It just took me about an hour to admit that to myself. What happened at the end was nothing more or less than what the audience *expected* would happen, what they'd been *told* would happen. There was no surprise. Yeah, I could turn in the script and it would pass muster with the studio because there were enough good scenes to sustain the story, but did I want to shoot something that was just okay?

I clicked through every trick and technique I knew, trying to figure out where I'd gone wrong and what I could do to fix it. Nothing worked. Then I tried *Turn it upside down*, and suddenly everything clicked.

I'd written the story around the assumption that, in her dreams, the catatonic woman was trying to keep something out. Turning that upside down meant asking, what if she was actually trying to keep something *in*?

What if her husband died before she had a chance to say goodbye? What if she could never let go of that moment, or him? What if everyone around her kept saying *You have to move on*, but she can't, so she holds on even tighter, locking his memory behind a door in her heart. Refusing to let go of that memory, she withdraws further and further from the world until it's all she has left, holding on as tight as she can because she believes she could never survive losing him twice.

That solved the problem, and in the new ending, rather than destroying what's on the other side of the door, he breaks it open to free the memory and the spirit of her dead husband. This allows them to finally say goodbye to each other, their love bridging the gap between life and death. When he asks her to keep going, to keep living, for him, for all the time they had together, his words also resonate with our protagonist. He realizes that he, too, must go on living despite his grief, because that's what his wife would have wanted.

I left the first half of the script intact because it was important to fool the audience into thinking there really *was* something terrible behind that door, and since I'd written that material at a time when I thought that was true, the scenes felt honest and didn't anticipate the new ending.

If there's a part of the story that's fighting you, turning it upside down can be useful across all kinds of storytelling.

When DC Comics asked me to reimagine Superman in a series of hardcover graphic novels, the challenge was immense because of the many times that the character had been reconsidered and reinvented over his seventy-five-plus-year history. How do you make something new or surprising when everyone already knows that Kal-El was sent to Earth when Krypton exploded as the result of natural processes that could be predicted but not controlled?

Turning it upside down meant asking: What if the destruction of Krypton *wasn't* an accident? What if it was deliberately destroyed by outside forces? A hit-job on a planetary scale? If so, then who did it, why, where did they go, and what does this mean for Superman's future? This question was key to the success of *Superman: Earth One*, which consistently ended up on the New York Times Best Sellers list.

When Marvel Comics asked me to come aboard as writer for the monthly run of *The Amazing Spider-Man*, the same problem emerged: How do you tell a story about Spider-Man that hasn't already been explored a million times? Everyone knows that Peter Parker got his powers when he was bitten by a spider that had been subjected to radiation, which allowed the spider to transfer its unique abilities.

Turning it upside down: What if the spider already *had* the power to transfer those abilities, and was desperately trying to get them to Peter before the radiation killed it? Which came first, the power or the radiation? If the former, then where did those powers originally come from, who would've wanted Peter to have them, and why? Digging into that question helped reinvigorate Marvel's core title, which was central to their plan to pull back from the brink of bankruptcy. Over that six-year run the book sold millions of copies worldwide, and this new examination of the Spider-Man mythos led directly to the creation of the Spider-Verse that was explored in later Marvel movies.

A few years later, Marvel decided to bring back Thor from a multi-year hiatus. In theory this pause in publication was undertaken to give the character a rest, but the truth is that quite honestly, the three other writers at the necessary level who were offered the title ran screaming into the night because no one knew what to do with him. Which is exactly why I took the assignment when the editors looked in my direction. If there are five projects on a table, and one of them is radioactive, it's the one nobody else wants, the horse that can't be ridden, *that's* the one I want. Every time.

In addition to changing his manner of speaking to something less corny, giving him a new outfit, bringing back Donald Blake, and developing a ton of new stories, one of the most important decisions I faced early on was deciding where to set Thor's home base of Asgard. The editors assumed I would put it atop a mountain (per mythology), or up in the clouds or in space, things that had been done before and left little room for new storytelling.

Turning that upside down: If the pattern in the past was to put Asgard somewhere high or otherworldly, then my immediate impulse was to put it in Oklahoma, in the middle of absolutely nothing. This would let us explore the interaction between humans and Norse gods in ways that had not been done before, opening the title to stories that would feel fresh and new. Despite concerns from the editors that this might not work, the approach returned the *Thor* book to the top ten best-selling comics every month for as long as I was writing it, and elements of that story were carried into the *Thor* movie, which I also worked on, and which earned half a billion dollars worldwide.

When confronted by a problem in one's art, the natural tendency is to seek solutions in small, incremental ways because you're nose-to-nose with the story, too close to gain perspective or see the problem for what it is. We think *what if I tweak this,* or *what if I adjust that* rather than taking a big, holistic view of the situation. Turning the problem upside down forces you to look at the story in an entirely new way. Done correctly, the result can come as a huge surprise to the audience because they've never played the *turn it upside down* game, while still feeling natural, because the flip is an extension of what's gone before. Following the logical consequences of that decision can then spin you off into all sorts of new possibilities.

So, when the work is fighting you, feels clichéd, or is too much the expected turn of events . . . turn it upside down to see what it looks like. You'll be amazed at what you see.

One final aside.

Ten paragraphs into this chapter, I mentioned trying "every trick and technique I knew." Having used those terms elsewhere, I should probably explain what I think those terms mean, and the differences between them.

A *trick* is something writers resort to when there's a glitch in the story and they lack either the talent or a sufficient understanding of the underlying problem needed to figure out a solution. So they use cheats, misdirection, or fireworks to *obscure* the problem rather than *solving* it, distracting the reader long enough for the writer to race ahead to another part of the story where they feel more sure-footed. Some refer to this as the "Look, a pony!" gambit. I prefer to call it waterskiing, wherein you keep moving as fast as you can because you know that if you slow down, what you're standing on won't support you.

I will confess to resorting to the occasional trick when the eleventh hour arrives and a producer/publisher needs the material *rightdamnitnow* and there's no time left for problem-solving. If I need a big act-out and the story is at a place that doesn't really allow for that, I'll have someone come in with a gun who doesn't really need to have one, make a threat, or plant a red herring (a clue that ultimately goes nowhere) in the hope that no one will remember it by the time the credits roll. I don't insert false jeopardy, but I do allow the reader or audience to see the shark fin cutting through the water, even if it never actually bites anyone. But I never consider it anything other than a temporary fix; before publication or filming, I always return to that part of the story in case time and distance have allowed a better solution to present itself.

Technique is a very different creature and comes out of a genuine understanding of the story, the characters, and the craft that is achieved only through years of experience. Techniques allow the writer to tilt the mirror just enough to look at the story with fresh eyes, as when an optometrist swings the phoroptor in front of your eyes and starts swapping out lenses. *Better like this, or better like **this**?*

Techniques are the tools we use to *express* our art; tricks are the bandages we use to *hide* the parts of the art that don't work when we lack the skill to understand them. At various times both can be useful as a way for talent to either manifest or protect itself, but mastering all the tricks in the world will not suffice if the talent is not there.

And that truth is one of the few things that can never be turned upside down.

TWO FOR THE PRICE OF FUN

G ood writers spend years learning the rules of their craft and figuring out how to make their work fit within them. Great writers challenge those assumptions and push themselves to create something new and extraordinary that surpasses the limits of their prior experiences. There are many methods to broaden one's horizons as a writer; one of the surest, but in many ways also one of the most difficult, is through collaboration.

Everything you have ever seen, heard, and experienced forms a lens in the middle of your forehead through which you see the world, a perspective shared by no one else. If diamonds are valuable because they are rare, how much more rare, and more valuable, is that point of view? When I hire a writer on a TV series, what I'm actually buying is the unique perspective they bring to the story. No one can write a Michael Chabon story as well as Michael Chabon. No one can write a Neil Gaiman story like Neil Gaiman can write it. No one can write a J. Michael Straczynski story as well as J. Michael Straczynski.

And no one can write a (fill in your name) story as well as you can.

That point of view is what makes writers irreplaceable. But if we never make the effort to look past our own perspective (which often requires acknowledging predilections and prejudices we'd rather not confront), that blinkered view can limit us as artists. Collaboration forces you to see the world through someone else's lens: you have to live inside their perspective, understanding their techniques and the incidents in their lives that shaped them as storytellers. The process keeps your creative muscles from becoming stiff, and can be done as a one-off, just for the experience and the learning curve, or it can be a lifetime arrangement.

Not everyone comes to the writing profession with equal skills in equal areas. Some writers are great at plot but suck at dialogue or characterization; others can craft strong dialogue or interesting characters but run into trouble when they try to create a compelling plot. Most writers keep plugging along in their own way, painstakingly learning the tools that will balance out their abilities, but some decide to expedite the process by finding writing partners who have skills in areas they lack.

This is especially true in television and film, which is why so many writing partners can be found listed in the credits. (Here's how to tell the difference between writers who collaborate as partners and writers who are brought in to do later drafts and thus don't write together. Under the terms of the Writers Guild of America, writers who work together as partners receive the *&* symbol in their on-screen credit, i.e., "Screenplay by John Smith & Tex Miller." Conversely, a writer hired to revise a script written by someone else receives *and* in their credit, "Screenplay by John Smith and Tex Miller.")

One of the best examples of successful collaboration I've encountered was practiced by two executive producers I worked under during the early days of my career, Jeri Taylor and the late David Moessinger. David's plots were always airtight, and while he excelled at creating conflict, the characters were not always as layered or well-considered as his plots, defined more by who they were *fighting* with than who they *were* or how they *felt*. Jeri's plotting and structure tended to be less about conflict than relationships, digging deep into the emotions and history of her characters. The dialogue that came out the other side of that process always felt natural and easy on the ears, but sometimes the individual scenes lacked the level of tension needed to make them feel vital. Individually they were strong writers, but together they could write rings around anybody else in town, and I include myself in that list. The strengths and weaknesses of one were perfectly balanced out by the other.

By contrast, trying to collaborate with someone who has the same skill sets as yourself can be tricky because humans are often very territorial. If both parties are equally good at creating dialogue, there will almost certainly be tugs-of-war over whose vision will be executed on the page. A few years ago, I collaborated with a friend on a pilot script for CBS and the process nearly ended in a duel. We were both world-builders who specialized in creating mythologies and unlikely character origins, so we were constantly tripping over each other during the writing process. And because we were good friends before starting the collaboration (and afterward, so the story has a happy ending), each of us expected the other to defer to our judgment out of friendship rather than letting the quality of the ideas win out. We made the mistake of dragging the friendship into the collaboration, and the only way we managed to avoid killing each other was by breaking out the various groups of characters. *Okay, you create all these people in* this *part of the world, I'll create everybody in this group over* here, *and we'll work our way toward the middle.* It worked well enough for us to finish the script, but the seams in the story were pretty obvious, and in the end the pilot was not picked up.

If you decide to seek out a collaborator for a project you're writing, you should do so early in the writing process rather than waiting until you've already written a ton of pages. Approaching your potential partner saying, "Hey, so I started writing this script, and it's mostly done, but I was wondering if you'd like to come in on it with me to see if we can make it better?" can come across badly because this reduces the other person to a hired hand helping out on *your* project, rather than the two of you creating something *together.* Successful collaborations begin at the ground level, allowing for equal participation.

It helps if your prospective collaborator is someone you know, but dragging a friendship into a collaboration can be as dangerous as dragging a collaboration into a friendship. I had been friends with the Wachowskis (creators of the Matrix films) for many years before Lana called one evening to discuss the idea of expanding into television and invited me up to San Francisco for a few days to bat some ideas around.

As we spent that weekend working in her home office, anyone walking past the door would have seen us talking about science fiction, literature, politics, free will vs predestination, and other subjects that interested us without noticing the secondary, almost subliminal conversation going on beneath the surface as we used that discussion to triangulate each other's strengths and weaknesses to determine if this would be a good fit.

192 J. MICHAEL STRACZYNSKI

We're both heavy researchers, but where Lana often goes to the research first and stitches together a character from there, I tend to start with the character then back into whatever research I need to support or invalidate what I created. Gifted with a twelve-story brain, Lana tends to dive deep into the sociological and philosophical underpinnings of whatever story is being developed. I come from a similar academic background, so I can go deep when sufficiently provoked, and we spent many hours discussing the role of speech in evolution, parallels between the growth of human culture and the development in nature of mycelium, and whether the meaning we give to our lives creates the narrative of our story or whether the narrative of our story is what gives us meaning.

There are people who, if you ask what time it is, will give you the history of the watch, and Lana and I are at least six of them. Seeing how we overlapped in that respect, I decided to pull back on the more high-flown aspects of the story in order to balance out the collaboration. Ceding the tall grass of Deep and Profound Meaning to Lana allowed me to lean in to a more visceral, pop-ish approach to developing the story and the characters that kept the house from levitating off the ground.

The only way to know how a car works is to look under the hood, and by the end of the weekend we'd looked under the hood well enough to understand each other's strengths, weaknesses, and creative language, which in turn allowed us to move on to more fulfilling and productive conversations. This is the fun part of collaboration.

The dangerous part of collaboration comes when you know each other's processes too well, which risks sabotaging the friendship *and* the collaborative process.

Joined now by Lilly, the Wachowskis and I spent months breaking out the characters and universe of the series that we had entitled *Sense8* (which was later sold as a series to Netflix) at their offices in Chicago, where they were in post-production on *Jupiter Ascending*, a feature they had written and directed for Warner Bros. So when they decided to hold two friends-and-family screenings of an early cut of *Jupiter*, I was invited to attend.

I'd planned on only watching the first screening so I could go back to my hotel to write, but during the film I saw a number of problems that stemmed from what I now understood of Lana's internal storytelling language. There are times when every artist is too far inside their own perception to see the flaws in the art—too deep in the fishbowl to see the water—and this was one such instance, so I came back for the second screening to make notes on what concerned me.

Afterward, while everyone else was having food and celebrating, I was in one of the offices typing up a list of problems that I felt had the potential to blow up the film with audiences and critics, along with some potential solutions. I didn't see any reason not to do this because I've always had a policy on every project I've ever produced that anyone can come at me at any time with concerns and questions, especially when there's still time to make whatever changes are needed to save the project.

But as it turned out, my internal language in regard to criticism was not the same as Lana's or Lilly's, and the flash of resentment and anger over my suggestion that there were *any* flaws in the movie nearly torpedoed the collaboration *and* the friendship. Seeing my distress afterward, producer Grant Hill, who had worked with the duo for many years, pulled me aside to explain that Lana and Lilly "do not entertain contrarian opinions."

This culminated in a tense meeting where the siblings said that the movie was perfect as it was, and that the six areas of concern I'd written up were utterly without merit. If we were to continue working together I would have to recant what they considered my "apocalyptic vision for the film."

So that's what I did, recalibrating the boundaries between the collaboration and the friendship. The tragedy is that when *Jupiter Ascending* came out, the same six concerns that I'd raised, all of which could have been easily fixed, were repeated almost verbatim by audiences and critics. A film that could have been made successful with a handful of small changes ended up as one of the year's least successful and most critically panned films, an Old Testament–level reckoning that deeply fractured our friendship.

Never bring the friendship into the collaboration, or the collaboration into the friendship. Be cordial but firm, know where the boundaries are, and expect no quarter based on prior relationships. A collaboration can only be successful if all parties involved agree that they will leave their personal ups and downs outside the office, and that the process will be professional, frank, and respectful, but also utterly ruthless.

WHAT'S IN THE BOX?

After moving to Los Angeles in 1981, I came to know about two dozen television writers who were considered to be at the top of their game. Some worked in animation, others in live action, but all were successful and highly sought after by networks and studios. By the late nineties, most of them were either out of the TV business entirely or were hustling for occasional assignments to keep their health insurance. So why did I end up the only one of our group who has been able to continue working month after year after decade? They didn't age out of the industry—most of them were still relatively young when they flamed out—nor was it a matter of talent. We were all pretty much on par in that respect. Wherefore then the difference?

I think the answer is all about the Box.

As their careers begin to falter, I suggested that they branch out into other venues, challenging them to write articles or novels or work in different genres. *Why not try mainstream dramas or comedies or true stories?* But each time, I bounced off the wall of *This is the kind of writer I am, this is the kind of story I tell, this is what I know I can do, this is the box I live in.*

And that's fine, as long as the industry wants what you write. But when the world and the business change and you don't, that's a problem. Afraid of trying new things that would push them outside their comfort zone, they lived in a box and they died in a box.

Because that's what boxes are *for*.

This is one of the reasons why, according to the Writers Guild, the median career span for a writer working in television is ten years. By that time the town has decided what sort of writer you are. Believing that they have defined you, that you have no surprises or new colors to show, they lose interest and walk off in search of the next shiny object.

In the real world, people can spend ten years training to be doctors or physicists, careers that will span the rest of their lives; writers can invest a lifetime preparing for their work only to have it *end* in ten years. Because the executives are *bored*. Because *you're* boring.

Correction: Because you've *let* yourself become boring.

A writing career can survive rejection, ridicule, starvation, and loneliness, but fear or complacency will kill it every time. The moment you stop pushing yourself past the border of what you think you can do, you're dead—you just don't know it yet. That knowledge comes later, and while this problem is more readily apparent in the film/TV business, it also applies to prose, as will be discussed in more detail in the last chapter.

One way to avoid this fate is what I call the Three Legged Stool Theory.

To survive as a writer one should always have at least three streams of revenue, and three forms of creative expression, going at all times. It keeps you fresh as an artist and financially stable. If one of the legs of the stool is shot out from under you, which will invariably happen at various stages of your career, you can lean back on the other two until a replacement can be found.

When I began my career as a writer, those three legs consisted of newspaper articles, fiction, and radio. When my efforts at fiction didn't work out as well as could be hoped for, I switched to animation, radio, and articles. Then as my career progressed, I switched to live-action television, comic books, and movies. In 2016, I announced my departure from writing comics, sawing off that leg of my own volition and replacing it with books (*Becoming Superman*, *Together We Will Go*, and this one).

But the value of the Three Legged Stool Theory goes beyond the purely financial.

It's said that in Feudal Japan, samurai were required to have at least one avocation beyond those required to be a good warrior. They were urged to pursue calligraphy, music, gardening, and art. Those who excelled at these pursuits also ended up being the best samurai, helping to make them focused and flexible. Stepping outside the expected paths can elevate us as artists.

Stagnation is death. If a farmer sows the same crops in the same field every year, he depletes the nutrients and the crops wither. This led to the development of crop rotation, which keeps the fields viable and constantly refreshed. The same idea applies to writing and creativity. Writing an article teaches you structure, which you can use in a short story; writing a short story teaches you dialogue, which you can use in a TV script; and writing a TV script gives you the discipline to write at greater length, which prepares you to write a novel or a movie. Writing a drama teaches you how to make compelling characters, which can make writing a science fiction film feel more realistic. Writing a science fiction movie teaches you how to incorporate bits of action or technology into a mainstream drama that can make it feel more contemporary. Everything feeds into everything else.

Moving your art through different permutations also makes you shiny in the eyes of buyers, a sidebar principle I refer to as the Prince from a Distant Land Scenario.

Comic book publishers deal with comic book writers all the time, and after a while they're not impressed.

TV networks deal with television writers all the time, and after a while they're no longer impressed.

Movie studios deal with screenwriters all the time, and that process is just what they expect it to be.

But:

A TV writer going to a comics publisher is a Prince from a Distant Land. A comics writer going to a movie studio is another Prince from a Distant Land. And a movie writer going to a TV network is also a Prince from a Distant Land. You become what they're not used to, something bright and shiny and new.

For as long as I've been a writer, I've been engaged in a process of constant rebirth and reinvention. I went from being a journalist, to an animation writer, to a live-action writer, to a comics writer, to a movie writer. I went from nonfiction to fantasy and science fiction (especially in *Babylon 5*), then switched it up by writing a historical drama (*Changeling*), flipped another 180 degrees to work on a horror story (*World War Z*), and my new novel, *Together We Will Go*, published almost simultaneously with this book, is a mainstream character drama written in epistolary format. Every time someone in the Industry tries to define me or pigeon-hole me as a particular kind of writer, I jump the other way, which amuses me and confuses the hell out of them.

I can't vouch for where I land on the talent scale, and on most days I generally land *under* the personality scale, but I can say with absolute confidence that the Prince From a Distant Land strategy is the primary reason why I've been able to continue working nonstop for almost forty years in an industry that generally only permits ten.

And if *I* can do it, god knows *you* can do it.

The more venues in which you work, the greater the opportunity to reinvent yourself as needed by jumping to another venue and becoming shiny all over again. Rather than spending your creative life in a box circumscribed by the same routine, you can go through life like a butterfly engaged in a cycle of perpetual rebirth, flying from one form to another, forever new, forever *shiny*.

THE THICK PLOTENS

E ven the most rudimentary writing book can describe the process of creating a plot, so we're not going to spend a lot of time on it here. Besides, we're in the "Staying a Writer" section, which means you've grown past the fundamentals to achieve some success as a writer. You've learned that a well-constructed plot is the lifeline upon which you can hang your action, character moments, and brilliant bits of dialogue. Plot is where story lives. When someone asks, "What's your story about?" you don't describe a bunch of random scenes; there's continuity in the telling, the plot, from A to B to C, the *Once upon a time* of it all.

The good thing about a strong basic plot is that it lets you tell your story in a straight line with no unwanted surprises.

The bad thing about a strong basic plot is that it tells your story in a straight line, with no surprises, wanted or otherwise.

Competent plotting represents the *beginning* of your journey as a writer, not the end. Sooner or later the need arises to craft plots that are more intricate or clever.

One of the most important lessons I learned about writing came while working on a weekly police procedural for producer David Moessinger, referenced earlier. By this point I'd written dozens of half-hour television episodes and story-edited scores more, so I thought I had a pretty fair idea about how to plot a story. But after turning in my first outline, I was surprised when David called me into his office, held up the outline, and said, "No, no, no, and by the way: no."

"Why?" I asked. "What's wrong with it?"

He sighed, sat back in his chair, and peered out at me over his reading glasses. "All of it, Joe. *All* of it."

I will confess that I bristled a little, because I was young and a bit full of myself. Besides, everything in the outline was stuff that we'd already discussed and he'd *approved*. So why was there suddenly a problem?

"You have our heroes going here, here, and *here* to get the information they need," David said.

"Right," I said. "They question the suspects and witnesses, just as we discussed."

"And they get the information."

"Well, yeah."

"That's the problem. The other characters just give them the information. The process needs to be difficult, people should refuse to cooperate, make themselves unavailable or even just lie. In fact, the more they lie the better because that adds tension and conflict, which the story currently lacks, and helps to establish them as red herrings to divert suspicion from the *real* suspect.

"This isn't about dryly accumulating clues and information, it's about fighting for every bit of data in scenes that showcase character and create conflict. But in your outline it's all *this* happened and *that* happened and the *other* thing happened, when it should be this *started* to happen, then *that* happened, so you try to regroup except this other thing happens, which you survive but then *this* gets in the way and everything goes sour. It's not and-and-and, it's *then, but,* and *except*."

He was right, of course. My only prior experience was in half-hour shows, an amount of screen time barely sufficient to establish your characters, hit your theme, deliver the exposition needed to understand what's going on, then get out clean; the structure needed to sustain an hour of storytelling had to be more complex, with twists, turns, feints, and, in the case of a mystery series, red herrings. (Or as one high-ranking Universal Studios executive used to say, with no one willing to risk correcting him, "false herrings.")

Another aspect of inserting this kind of conflict is that it tends to be more emotionally true. In a situation where there's been a murder there's a tendency for everyone to lie for different reasons. The guilty lie for all the obvious reasons, and the innocent may be tempted to lie to avoid being blamed for something they didn't do.

Plotting is about logical truths.

Storytelling is about emotional truths.

And sometimes those are the same thing, and sometimes they are not.

Throwing roadblocks in front of your characters forces them, and by consequence you, to be more ingenious in pursuing the story. The bigger the boulder blocking their path, the stronger they are for having moved it, especially if the boulder doesn't come with a ready-made flaw that renders it easily broken.

So, once you've reached the end of your story, go back to the beginning and open fire, being relentless as you try to punch holes in your story logic. Question every choice, every decision, every twist and turn to ensure that it's bulletproof. This doesn't just apply to the big moves of your story; scrutinize *all* the choices made by your characters, down to the smallest detail. Did they choose the smart way, or the most convenient path for you as the storyteller? If the latter, are there other possibilities that might be more interesting?

And answering that question sometimes involves listening to the voice in your head that seems counter-intuitive to the step-by-step rigor of conventional plotting.

One of my earliest choices while producing *Babylon 5* was that a character named Londo Mollari would kill his emperor in order to avert war and save those he cares about. Londo was a likeable character but utterly ruthless when necessary, so there was no question that he was capable of doing what the story required.

Under Mollari was his assistant Vir Cotto: shy, naïve, good-natured, and decent, the sort of man for whom the phrase *he'd never hurt a fly* was invented. Also: *raised by mice*. But when it came time for me to finally write the assassination scene, Vir turned to me in my head and said, "You're making a mistake."

"What do you *mean*, I'm making a mistake?" I shot back. "I'll remind you that I created you!"

"Doesn't matter. You're still doing a dumbness. If anyone's going to kill the emperor, even if it's by mistake, it should be me."

"But Mollari's the logical choice given the plot."

"No, he's the *easy* choice. If he kills the emperor it's just business as usual—it won't leave a mark. Will that get your overall story arc where it needs to go? Sure, but so will this. You're going down the *this-happens-then-this* road because it's easier than the *this-but-except* road. If *I* kill the emperor it's a surprise, it's a twist in the plot, and unlike Londo I'll grieve, I'll have remorse, and you can dine off that for at *least* six episodes."

The more I thought about it, the more I realized that he (or whatever part of my brain was playing "Vir" for purposes of this conversation) was right. So in the middle of a sentence I went the other way and had Vir do the deed, and it became one of the strongest moments in the entire series.

My only regret is that I didn't have that revelation earlier in the process, because making *that* decision at *that* moment meant that I wasn't able to layer in all the little beats that would have led up to it. A big part of storytelling is about playing fair with the audience, meaning that all the elements needed to see where the story's going are there from the first line, but only snap into focus as more of the story is revealed. Ideally, an audience should be able to back up the movie or return to page one and see that all the clues were right there in plain sight.

Not playing fair with the audience means that sudden character turns, plot twists, or revelations come out of nowhere, unsupported by prior events, often directly contradicting everything the audience knows about these characters. It's okay for a surprise ending to feature a startling turn of events or characterization, provided that the writers have done their job right. The turn should feel emotionally true because they've used bits of foreshadowing to show that there was more to the character than met the eye, hinting at a degree of decency (or cruelty) that was just waiting for the right moment to manifest itself. The bigger the change in the character, the more it should feel like a natural outgrowth of everything that went before.

In a shock ending, none of those rules apply: the characters do what they do not because it makes sense or was established, but because the writers don't care what went before. They're interested in shocking the audience, or they've written themselves into a corner and don't know how to write themselves out of it so they just blow it all up. The characters do what they're *told* rather than doing what is emotionally true.

Emotion drives plot. Emotion *is* plot, providing the links of causality and consequence that turn a series of incidents into a story.

The king died, then the queen died is incident.

The king died, then the queen died of grief is a story.

Find those emotional connections and stick to them as you develop your stories. Play fair with the audience, treat the characters honorably while being ruthless with your decisions, and never let logical truths blind you to emotional truths that can still get you where you're going in your plotting with even greater personal consequence.

LIVING (OR AT LEAST SURVIVING) THE WRITING LIFE

Sustaining a long-term career as a writer is about more than credits, clippings, publication, production, and, one hopes, awards and applause. (Though they definitely make the road a little easier.) There's the whole messy but necessary business of actually living life that has to be factored into the equation, how we handle relationships and how we react to failure, success, and all points in between.

Like every carbon-based life-form reading this, I've had my share of ups and downs when it comes to relationships, and there are a lot of things I wish someone had said to me years ago about finding the balance between relationships and the artistic impulse. Since everything else in this volume is written as a conversation between me and thee, fellow writer, that's probably how this chapter would also have gone. But of all the regrets that still haunt me today, the greatest are the things I could have said, *should* have said, to those I loved, or who loved me, had I known which words to say.

So I'd like to address myself for a moment to the one sitting beside you: your significant other, your wife, boyfriend, husband, partner, or family member. Your *Person*, whatever that means at the time you read this. Hand over this book and leave the room for a bit. We'll get back to you later. Meanwhile, get gone. Seriously. Git.

Okay. Are they gone? Good.

First: my sympathies. You are involved with, in love with, married to, or linked by blood to a *writer*. They could've been a cut-purse, an extortionist, a pyromaniac, a serial killer, or a congressperson, but no, they chose the artist's life. (Technically it chose them, but we'll get to that bit in a minute.) It is a thorny, difficult, and often painful road, so let me try to move some of the thorns aside so you can better see where you're walking.

Let me first get the hard part out of the way.

If your Person has been able to forge a career in writing, it's because they are passionate about the work and driven to succeed, and that drive, that *art*, will always take center stage in his or her life. Yes, they love you to the best of their ability; they miss you when you are gone and rejoice in your presence; they dedicate the work to you, celebrate your patience and your support; their love is so deep and profound that they would step in front of a bus or a bullet for you, and they would do it gladly. They *love* you.

But in their heart, no matter what they say to the contrary, they know that the work will always come first, and they don't know how to express that without hurting you, afraid you won't understand. Because it's not *about* you, it's about the relentless voice that won't let them rest until they put in that day's required hours behind the keyboard; it's about the joy of the writing and the terrible, relentless hunger that constantly tears at them, pushing them to go further, to test the limits of what they can do.

For your Person, it's not about who loves who most. It's about beating death. Overcoming mortality. Leaving a mark. It's about saying *I existed, I was* here, *this is who I was, what was important to me, and how the world looked to me before the void reclaimed me.* Death terrifies us all, and without the certainty of a heaven, a hell, or an afterlife, the only immortality a writer can hope to achieve comes through the work.

You are not dealing with a competitor for your Person's affection.

You are dealing with someone who is afraid of the dark, and equally fearful of ever having to confess that.

Writing is how they make sense of the world, and of *themselves*; it's a form of self-definition. Writing isn't just what they *do*, it's who they *are* at a personal, primal, *cellular* level. Tell a writer that he or she can't write anymore, and there will be a person-shaped puff of smoke like a Road Runner cartoon as they simply vanish from creation.

Every minute of every day, they're terrified that it's all going to stop; that the next piece won't sell, that the words won't come, that the train will stop, that someone will come in the night to confiscate their Writer's Card and destroy their carefully crafted self-definition. If asked, they will of course deny this. They are lying.

So, given that Olympus-sized psychodrama, what can you do, and what should *they* do, to level the playing field between you so nobody feels they're being taken advantage of or insufficiently considered?

It starts with giving them space. Yes, it may look like they're working at home, right there in the next room, but that's just an illusion. In reality they are somewhere in the vicinity of Proxima Centauri, rocketing through the universe in search of the Meaning of Life. While they are on that voyage, it's vital to let them travel without interruption as much as possible. Yes, that's unfair and no fun because you want to talk to them and tell them about your day or ask a question or find out what to make for dinner or why the dog is on fire. This is necessary even when they're not actually typing anything, because that's the stage during which they decide what they want to write next in the instant before they lean forward and fingers meet keyboard.

There is a famous cartoon drawn by Mark Twain that shows him sitting with his eyes closed, feet up on the desk, captioned *Just because I'm not writing doesn't mean I'm not writing*. It may look like daydreaming on the outside, but on the inside . . . well, okay, it's daydreaming, but it's *constructive* daydreaming.

One of the most famous poems in English literature is "Kubla Khan" by Samuel Taylor Coleridge, notable for its rich language and imagery, the brilliance of its sound and its structure, and the fact that it was never finished. According to Coleridge, the poem hit him all at once, so he rushed to the desk and began writing in white heat. Just as he hit the midpoint there came a knock at the door. By the time he returned to his desk, the rest of the poem had fled his thoughts; it was gone, just *gone*. That thirty-second interruption cost English literature a poem that might have become one of the Greats.

Granted that we are not all Coleridge, and there's long been suspicion that various mind-altering chemicals may also have been part of the equation, but the principle still applies.

The trade-off for you respecting their time is that if you've agreed that the window for creation is from 7 until 9 p.m., is they can't complain if you come in at 9:15 to engage them in conversation. (I added fifteen minutes because there's always one last cool sentence that shows up just as you run out of time and dares you to write it down.) In return for you respecting the writing window, your Person must respect the importance of making time for you and for each other. Writing creates its own unique form of inertia: an object at desk tends to remain at desk unless and until acted upon by an equal and opposite *you said we'd go to the beach today what the hell is wrong with you?*

There will always be more that needs to be written, another deadline that needs to be met, so it's easy to find reasons to stay at the keyboard, but attention *must* be paid to the living of life. While making *Babylon 5*, I was invited by the air force (a number of officers were fans of the show) to ride in an F-16. *I'd love to*, I said, *but I can't; I have too much writing to get done.* A year later, some fans at NASA invited me to the Kennedy Space Center in Florida to watch the launch of a space shuttle, not from the usual seats, but from a position *just* outside the *Get any closer and the engines will fry you* range.

My reply: *Love to, can't, gotta write.*

I have spoken those words many times over the years, and looking back I regret the many once-in-a-lifetime experiences that I allowed to slip past. I miss the places I have not visited because doing so would take me from the work, the parties unattended, the fireworks unseen, the lips unkissed . . . *Hey, sweetie, I'm going to be in your part of town later tonight, how about I swing by and we frolic like bunnies?*

Love to, can't, gotta write.

Idiot.

Make dates and keep them. Create rewards for getting the work done that involve going out and seeing the world and *doing* things. Neither of you wants to hit sixty looking at a cabinet of awards on one side, and on the other, a life consisting of a catalogue of missed opportunities.

Having established that writing is a form of self-definition, it follows that criticism—especially when it is seen as unfair—can be devastating to writers because it can be perceived as a credibility attack on their very reason for existence. My work has received literally thousands of reviews in dozens of countries, and the damnable thing is that I can call to mind very few of the positive notices. But I remember all the bad reviews. Right down to the punctuation.

When your Person is stung by a bad review, soft words will not help. Nor will saying *He doesn't know what he's talking about, he's not qualified to offer an opinion, he's a jerk, don't listen to him*. The only thing you *can* do can only be done when a good review appears. That's the moment when you have to say, *That's great, sweetie, but take it with a grain of salt, because if you believe the good reviews then you have to believe the bad ones too. If you keep them both at arm's length, they can't hurt you. If there are any specific observations that you think are useful, great, take them to heart, then kick the rest of it to the curb.*

Then when the bad reviews come, remind them of that conversation. It won't take away all of the sting, but it will make the process a little less painful.

From time to time, your Person may ask you to critique something he or she has written. This is perilous territory in any relationship, and you will be torn between telling your Person exactly what you think, or soft-pedaling your reaction to avoid upsetting them. Doing the former risks causing offense, and doing the latter can lead your Person to decide that there's no point to asking your opinion since you'll just tell them what you think they want to hear. They need to know they can go to you for an honest opinion.

It's especially difficult to walk that line when you don't know the subtext. Perhaps your Person wants to show you something they've finished because they think it's amazing, so they can see that same amazement reflected in your eyes; or maybe they've come to you because they feel that something in the story is broken and hope that you can see the solution. Unfortunately, there's no way for you to know which of those is in play as they hand you the pages. *Read this and tell me what you think.*

Or, stated a tad more honestly, *I made you a bear trap—step in it and tell me what you think!*

Whatever a writer may *think* he or she wants in such a critique, what they *need* is honesty, but not everyone can handle that. If you give a negative opinion and for the next few days find the emotional weather in your relationship only slightly colder than the Arctic Shelf, you know what you are (or aren't) dealing with. So here are some ways to finesse your critique without being false.

Let's say that you genuinely love the latest piece of writing by your Person. While this is absolutely the best-case scenario, you must force yourself to find *something* corrective, however small, to mention during your critique.

I really loved this, it's so much fun, the characters are great, I totally didn't see the end coming but when you get there it all makes sense. The only part where I bumped a little was when Beatrice blows up at her husband during their argument on page 17. She's so clever throughout the rest of the story, it seems like she might rein this in a little so she doesn't tip her hand when she goes for revenge later in the story.

Here's why this is important.

I'm not a director, nor do I have any desire to *be* a director, because it means getting up early and I have no wish to inflict that version of myself on people who have done nothing to earn that sort of horror. But I have directed on occasion, and during the first day of shooting I always make it a point to give the actor a note about something I didn't like about his or her performance. Doesn't matter if I have to invent a critique, I do it every time, because once the actor recognizes that I'm willing to give them a negative note, they become more willing to accept subsequent praise as truth. They flourish in the knowledge that I'm not just being nice or trying to make them happy.

Commenting on one thing that you didn't like or felt could be improved will help your Person accept that you are being authentic in your reaction. (So once you finish reading this section, be sure to tear out this page so your Person won't know what you're up to. Say you spilled coffee on it. If you don't have any at hand, for god's sake brew some fast.)

Rather than a work of undiluted genius, let's now pretend that the piece your Person asked you to read isn't up to snuff. I won't say awful because if your Person is selling their work, they're not going to be turning out drivel. The intriguing thing about writers is that each time they go up one notch in their work, they rarely slip back down again. They can lock up where they are, but falling backward to a prior level of quality is quite uncommon. So the work is functional, but it's not what it needs to be or should be. What then?

Once again, honesty is the best policy, but as with the preceding example, there is wisdom in tempering that critique with a positive note about something you genuinely liked. (For more on this approach, see the part about constructive criticism in the chapter on workshops.) This gives your Person a light to move toward as they work their way through the parts that need to be fixed.

If your Person can trust you as a fair arbiter, that you will speak the truth without trying to be harsh or unduly nice, that you can see the positive and the negative in the work and address them equally, he or she will see you not as an outsider to the work but as an ally, and that is a magnificent gift to someone engaged in such a solitary profession. Your Person *wants* to share their joy with you, and it will mean everything for them to know that you will create a safe place for them to do that.

One last point before I let you go.

Some say that an artist's life is one of feast and famine. This is not entirely correct. It's more accurate to say that it's one of feast-famine-famine-famine-feast-famine-feast-famine-famine-famine-evenmorefamine-alittlefeast-ohcrapFAMINE. So there are going to be times when your Person's belief in themselves and their art will be profoundly tested. As bills come in that can't be paid and self-doubt cripples output, your Person will move beyond your reach, trapped in their own personal hell of perceived failure. Give them room. Suffering our way into renewed resolve is sometimes just how writers work. All your Person really needs during this time is to know that you believe in them, and that you will be there for them when they come out the other side of the nightmare.

Okay, you can call your Person back into the room for some concluding thoughts.

Hey, hi . . . we missed you while we were talking. It was nothing earth-shattering, but it was good to get a few things out in the open.

Sorry about the coffee stains.

We were just discussing the ups and downs of the writing business, and the failures that sometimes come along with the successes, which is why it's essential to be careful with your finances. For every dollar that comes in from the writing, you should put fifty cents into a savings account and for god's sake don't touch it for vacations or home theaters. That money should be considered sacrosanct, to be touched *only* in times of fiscal stress. This is essential not only so you can pay the rent, but so you can follow your talent without compromise.

In 1959, Rod Serling wrote an installment of *Playhouse 90* entitled "The Velvet Alley" about a television writer's meteoric rise and tragic fall. At one point, after having moved into an expensive home to distract himself from the fiery cataclysm that is becoming his personal life, the protagonist is sitting in the backyard with his agent, who delivers a Jeremiad that every writer should take to heart. Paraphrased for brevity, he says that "the thing about writing for television is that they bring you out here and pay you all this amazing money for what you do. Then slowly, gradually, your lifestyle rises to the point where you *need* that money on a regular basis to sustain it all.

"And then they threaten to take it away.

"And then they own you."

That is the Velvet Alley, and the only way to avoid ending up stuck at the bad end of that alley is by being careful with your money. Try not to put yourself in a position where you have to say yes to something you would never otherwise do because you're out of cash. Be wise. Be prudent. *Beware*.

Since the next chapter, the last in our extended conversation, is also a warning, I want to conclude this chapter on a gentler note, a topic writers rarely talk about because it so rarely comes up.

I want to talk about joy.

When we're writing, we're usually in a safe place, alone with the words. But when we're *not* writing we often find ourselves in a state of near-constant panic, worried about whether or not we're talented enough to get us where we want to go, if we're really as talented as we've been *telling* everyone we are without actually *knowing* we are.

Getting away from the work to attend dinners and other social obligations rarely helps since the conversation eventually turns to what you do for a living. *What are you working on now? Is it any good? Have you sold anything? Are you a Somebody or are you a Nobody, in which case I should go get another drink.*

Even sleep is no escape, which is why many writers are insomniacs. We spend all day making connections between things because that's how stories happen, and that process doesn't stop when you close your eyes at night; it turns inward and suddenly the circus comes to town. It's just awful. You turn off the lights, climb into bed, and just as you start to doze off a story idea will flash into view, or a bit of dialogue, a fragment of a song or a poem, or a better way of shading the meaning in a scene you *technically* stopped working on a few hours ago, so you switch on the bedside light (or go into the other room to avoid annoying your partner) to scribble it all down. Then you go back to bed, and just as you settle in another fragment comes to mind and the cycle starts all over again.

When we're not making money from our work there's no opportunity for joy because we're panicked that we'll never work again; when we *do* get an assignment there's no room for joy because now we have to get the work done; and when we're done there's *still* no time for joy because we're back to worrying if we'll ever work again.

So where *does* joy enter the equation? Whence happiness in the writer's life?

Yes, the work is important, so you set aside 4–6 a.m. every morning to write in solitude before the rest of the house wakes up. But it's equally important to schedule time to watch movies, play games, go for a walk, sit outside in the shade, and tell those you love how much they mean to you. Make time to celebrate victories large and small. Anyone who suffered through Psychology 101 is familiar with the term Pavlovian Response: you ring a bell, then immediately feed a dog some treats. Do this enough times and the dog associates the sound of the bell with the food, and will salivate the second it hears the bell.

Any time you get or finish an assignment or write something on spec, you *must* reward yourself with a treat. (And don't say *I'll celebrate when I sell it*; that's a perfectly fine reason for another celebration later, but it doesn't preclude acknowledging that by finishing the present work you have accomplished something of value.) Go to a favorite restaurant or eat a dessert that you only have when you're celebrating something, so your brain knows that if it wants that treat again you'll have to finish the next project.

You can also reward yourself for completing a project by buying something to commemorate the occasion, even if it's just a cheap little gift that you can put on your desk as a reminder, when completion of a future project seems impossible, that you can do it. Cover your desk in mementos of all the finish lines you've crossed, and find joy in surveying those accomplishments.

And make time to love.

As the years pass, your non-writing Person will be the most important individual in your life, supporting and advising and being there for you. Tell them that you love them every chance you get. Invent opportunities if necessary, but get it done. You stand as a writer on the shoulders of your predecessors, but you stand as a *person* only insomuch as the one you love stands with you. It's fine to let them see your passion for your work, but don't neglect the passion and the affection you have for them as well. One needn't preclude the other, *ever*.

Finally, as noted at the very beginning of this book, if you've had any measure of success as a writer, it behooves you . . . no, it *requires* you to reach back and help the next person up the ladder, not just because it's the right thing to do but also because there is much joy to be found in this. Go back to your old high school or college and talk to the students there who are eager to pursue their own dreams. Mentor protégés. Recommend new writers to publishers, give workshops, do whatever you can to let the next bunch know that it's possible to succeed as a writer. Because that's really all they need, just to know that success is possible, that it *can* be done, that the blood and the work and the isolation and the fear can be worth it in the end.

One can go far on hope.

You did.

Now give it to the next person in line.

CONCLUDING THOUGHTS: TOUCHING THE WORLD

On several occasions, I had the honor to meet, converse with, interview, and have dinner with Ray Bradbury. My introduction to science fiction came courtesy of the Holy Trinity—Bradbury, Isaac Asimov, and Arthur C. Clarke—and I read everything I could get my hands on by those authors, Bradbury in particular. To this day I still remember the sense of wonder I experienced reading *The Martian Chronicles* for the first time. Despite having always been ridiculously careful in how I treat my books, I reread *R Is for Rocket*, *S Is for Space*, *The Golden Apples of the Sun*, *The Illustrated Man*, and *I Sing the Body Electric* so many times that the covers fell off.

Our first encounter came courtesy of a weekly radio show in Los Angeles that I hosted for five years called *Hour 25*, which led to subsequent meetings, conversations, and dinners before the broadcast. (The station, KPFK-FM, couldn't afford to pay guests to appear on any of their shows, so buying them dinner before or after the broadcast seemed the least I could do.)[1] The only time this bit me in the ass was when we had dinner before the show with mutual friend Norman Corwin, and Ray—who had probably just a tick more wine than was probably wise—went on to spend

---

1 Another occasional guest, author Dean Koontz, once gave me the shortest but also most profoundly relevant answer to the question "What drives you to write all the time?" that I have ever received. His four-word reply: "Once poor, never rich."

a good chunk of the broadcast trying to convince me that the United States would be eminently better off if it were run by the Walt Disney Corporation.

During these conversations, I slowly and with profound sadness began to realize that Ray had disengaged with the world, that he had pulled down the curtain on the present in deference to setting his stories in a nostalgic 1940s America that now existed only in his own mind. He let the world engage with *him*, through fans and friends who came to offer their respect for his work, and he was unfailingly generous in encouraging others to engage with the world, but when it came to his own creative impulse, the river had stopped flowing the other way. The man who once looked out his window to see a world rife with anti-intellectualism and censorship, and took his skills to the bleeding edge to challenge that system in *Fahrenheit 451*, had closed the window and settled into the somnolence of *Everything was so much better before, things are far too confusing now, I live in Greentown, a place of gazebos and boys with fishing poles standing beside placid streams and everybody is fair and did I mention that the country would be doing just great right now if we turned it all over to the Walt Disney Corporation?*

There are times we all say something that reveals more than we'd intended, and the Disney observation was one such revelation.

There are two things you will always find in Disneyland (or Disney World, or Disney Mars, which you just *know* they've already designed), and one thing that is noticeably absent. In Disneyland you will find the past, in castles and kingdoms and princes and princesses, in haunted ancient mansions and re-creations of fabulous places that once were but are no more. And you will find the future prophesied in displays of high technology, gleaming steel, and glittering screens through which we receive glimpses of far-flung, distant worlds and galactic empires.

What you will *not* find is the present. Because the present is fractious, full of conflict and uncertainty, moral ambiguities, and challenges to the status quo.

The past gives us the lure of an idyllic time and place that never really existed, but which we still long for, an escape from the complexity of the present moment; the future gives us a point on the horizon toward which we may travel, an escape from the narrow confines of the present into the place where our dreams await us. The present just leads to arguments and politics and nobody has a good time.

Like Disneyland, Ray had dialed out of the present to embrace a nostalgic past or dream about a bright future waiting to be realized, and for the average person, there's nothing wrong with that. But for a writer it's suicide when it becomes a lifestyle, limiting where the creative impulse can, and *must*, take us. The moment a writer disengages from the present world, something vital is lost. This, I feel, is what happened with much of Ray's later stories, none of which attained the same level of greatness as his earlier works. And just to be clear, I'm not attributing that downward incline to age. Many other writers of his generation were able to produce fresh, vital, relevant work in their considerably later years, including Norman Mailer, Henry Miller, Studs Terkel (who received the Pulitzer Prize at age seventy-three), and the aforementioned Norman Corwin, who produced socially relevant books and programs well into his nineties.

Shutting the door to the world and refusing to engage is a *choice*, and Ray made it. I do not question his profound wisdom or his reasons for making that decision, I'm just pointing out that at some point it got made, and made *hard*.

(Oddly, I had a similar conversation while hosting *Hour 25* with writer and TV celebrity Steve Allen. A masterful jazz musician as well as a fine actor, Allen took the position—and I still fail to understand the rationale behind this—that rock music was not music. He wasn't saying it was *bad* music, or music that was not to his liking; he insisted, repeatedly and with growing annoyance the more I pressed him on the point, that it wasn't music *at all*, period, end of discussion. From this position I think we can infer what aspect of Disneyland was Mr. Allen's favorite.)

Choosing not to engage with the world is a Velvet Alley of a very different but no less destructive nature.

Whether you're a new writer or an established writer, a plumber or a doctor, staying in the moment, engaging the world, and being mindful and present can be incredibly difficult. It's easy to fall into nostalgia or try to daydream away the problems of the present without actually addressing them.

If you're an older, established writer and there's nothing on your music playlist that's newer than the last fifteen years, you haven't got a playlist, or you don't know what a playlist *is* . . . if you haven't challenged your beliefs and listened to the opinions of those who are coming onto the stage next, you have disengaged.

Being Disneyland is easy.

Being present is hard, but desperately necessary if you want to *continue* writing anything of value and relevance. Despite the possibility of pain, you must remain vulnerable to experience and open to the world, to new ideas, and to experiencing the world directly, even when it scares you. Be present, mindful, *aware*. Never settle today for what you thought or wrote the day before, and question everything, especially the things you most fiercely accept as true.

The writer's task is to engage with the world and report back on what you see. Yes, that perception may be couched in the trappings of fantasy, but there must be some present truth, some present *beauty*, at its core. You must be willing to touch passion, endure the fire and the pain, and tell the rest of us what it was like. You needn't accept every idea you encounter—being open doesn't mean setting aside your critical facilities—but at least be aware of those ideas. Spend time listening to people outside your demographic. In the last several years, I've had the chance to get to know folks in the often maligned and disregarded categories of Millennials and Generation Z, and I sincerely believe that these are the people who will save the world, if only because they have less to lose than most of those who preceded them.

Everyone you meet is a story; every place you go is a setting for a tale as yet unwritten; every sentence spoken, however casual, can trigger a revelation or a revolution that will shake the world to its foundation. And everywhere there is beauty. Yes, there is darkness and violence and much worse, but there are gemstones amid the gravel, charity and kindness and honor and decency, and the world needs you to see it and tell us about it.

Because through you, the world dreams.

And if we do it just right, the next generation *becomes* that dream.

This volume has taken the position, often and at great length, that when it comes to the writing profession there are no guarantees. This is the one exception, because if you cannot live in the present and fearlessly engage with the world, sooner or later you will fall, and fail, and that will be the story of you.

Take chances.

Chase your dreams.

Pursue love.

Tell your stories.

Open your heart.

Be vulnerable.

Be engaged.

Be *true*.

That is the secret.

There is no other.

Good luck.

ACKNOWLEDGMENTS

My thanks and appreciation to the following: Emma Parry, Agent Extraordinaire at Janklow & Nesbit, for finding a home for this book; publisher Glenn Yeffeth for opening the door to that home and making me feel welcome; editor Robb Pearlman for keeping me honest and making sure I didn't break anything valuable; and my late mentor and friend Norman Corwin, who guides me to this day through his words and the example of his life.

My thanks also to Jason Shankel, Jonathan D. Gibson, Karthik Bala, Anna Shimeki, Matthew Murray, Dianne Hackborn, and Orion Perenyi for their support.

INDEX

ABOUT THE AUTHOR

J. Michael Straczynski has written for every known medium except poetry, at which he sucks. As a writer, producer, and show-runner, his television credits include over three hundred produced scripts for such series as *The Twilight Zone, Jeremiah, Babylon 5*, and *Sense8*. His work in film covers *Changeling* (for which he was nominated for a British Academy Award [BAFTA] for Best Screenplay), *Thor*, and *World War Z*, among others. In the comics world, he has written nearly four hundred comics for Marvel, DC, and other comics publishers that have sold over thirteen million copies worldwide. His Hugo-nominated autobiography, *Becoming Superman* for Harper Voyager, received glowing reviews from such venues as the *New York Times*, the *Washington Post*, the *Wall Street Journal*, NPR, and the BBC.

His most recent work includes *Together We Will Go*, a novel from Simon & Schuster; a new line of comics for Artists Writers & Artisans; and two original audio-drama series, *Dunwich* and *The Far Horizon*, for Penguin Random House. He is currently teaching Advanced Television and Film Writing for the Masters Degree in Screenwriting Program at San Diego State University.

Straczynski has won the Inkpot Lifetime Achievement Award, the Ray Bradbury Award, the Eisner Award, the Hugo Award (twice), the Saturn Award, the E Pluribus Unum Award from the American Cinema Foundation, the Space Frontier Award, the Christopher Foundation Award, the GLAAD Media Award for Outstanding Drama Series, and his graphic novels have consistently ended up on the New York Times Best Sellers list.

A terrible singer, an abysmal dancer, and utterly hopeless in fashion or conversation, he travels the world to speak about writing at seminars and conventions even when not technically invited, and calls Los Angeles his home despite repeated requests from city officials to knock it off because it drags down the housing market.